Starting out in the pharma industry

Essential knowledge for life scientists

Dr CF Harrison

Harrison Scientific

Introduction

Many of us eventually decide that we are no longer interested in the academic system. This might be due to a dislike of working at the lab bench, a lack of interest in chasing publications, or simply a desire to earn a more reliable income. The usual response to this problem is "go into industry", an excellent idea in principle but one which is made much harder by all of the unfamiliar terminology, requirements, and job descriptions.

This book will help to explain the many complexities of the pharmaceutical industry: the processes, the expectations, the skills you need to know and the careers you can enter – all laid out in an informative and jargon-free manner.

*First, we'll provide an introduction to the entire **drug development and manufacturing process**.*
We cover how a drug goes from chemical entity to a final pharmaceutical; we describe how batches of drugs are made, checked, and released to the market; we look at the marketing process, pharmacovigilance, and how processes change over time. Regardless of your role, this overview will help you understand the wide range of options in the industry.

*Next, we will cover industry **expectations**.*
This includes the type of knowledge you should be picking up during the first few weeks and months and how you should go about doing so; the attributes you should be cultivating to make a good impression on your co-workers and managers; and how to work effectively with your manager.

*Following this we cover **necessary industry skills**.*
These are the skills you need to know to succeed. How to communicate effectively, how to attend and run a meeting (yes, there will be a lot of meetings); how to organise all of the incoming information and how to plan projects. We also look at the best approach to take when things inevitably go wrong.

*Later we look at **starting and building your pharmaceutical career**.*
We provide a description of the most common entry roles taken by life scientists moving into industry, alongside a number of steps you can use to develop your career beyond that initial step. Finally there is a terminology list, explaining not only those terms **highlighted** throughout the text but a multitude of others related to pharmaceuticals.

This book is thus an excellent resource for those who have started or want to start in the pharmaceutical industry. Want to excel in your new career? Then read on...

Table of Contents

Chemical to blockbuster: Getting a drug to market

There is a long, complicated road to be followed before a new pharmaceutical can be sold on the market and used to treat patients – and the complexity doesn't go away after approval. This road is often a mystery to those who are beginning in the pharmaceutical industry – it has strange jargon, jobs you've never heard of before, legal requirements which seem to make no sense. This section will help to ease some of that confusion and give you an overview of the pharmaceutical lifecycle. From early development to regulatory approval and then all the way on through manufacture, pharmacovigilance and follow-up stability, on to change evaluations, this section will help you understand the many different processes involved in bringing a drug to the patient.

Research and development

Every pharmaceutical on the market began with an idea. The idea varies – it could be something like 'this protein seems to control cell replication' (leading to anti-cancer therapies), 'I wonder if our drug works on this other disease?' (leading to expanded **indications**) or even just 'that other drug is making a pile of money' (leading to **generics** and **me-too drugs**). Getting from an idea to a product, however, is a long and expensive road – and this road begins at the development phase.

The development stage consists of the research work which is done prior to clinical trials, a stage which includes *in vitro* work, cell culture studies, and animal experiments. This stage is usually the most familiar to those coming from academia, as research and development is the core of the university experience.

The first step in making a new medicine is the identification of the **target**, the protein or process which is (a) involved in the disease and (b) which you would like to modify with your drug. Ideas for targets will come from basic research, both academic and corporate. It is very common to see small **spin-off companies** set up by academic entrepreneurs with a focus on commercialising a new technology or potential target identified during their own basic research work.

Once a target has been identified, a drug which binds to and affects the target needs to be found. This process is usually done via **screening**, trialling many hundreds of thousands of options to identify those which have an acceptable affinity for the target. Screening systems use compound libraries (many small molecules of different shapes and sizes in a series of plastic microtiter plates) or phage display libraries (many different protein binding domains expressed on the surface of viral vectors). In both cases the process will identify what compounds bind, how well they do so, and whether this binding alters the action of the target.

Development stage	Number of compounds being investigated	Stage duration (years)
Drug discovery	5000 – 10000	4
Preclinical studies	250	1.5
Clinical trials	5	5
Regulatory approval	1	1.5

The number of compounds under investigation drops dramatically with each succeeding stage of drug development. Of the thousands of candidate molecules only a tiny fraction will reach regulatory approval.

The successes from this stage, known as **hits**, will then be modified to improve their attributes – small molecules will have differing functional groups swapped around, biologicals will undergo rounds of targeted mutagenesis. This occurs alongside a series of *in vitro* and *ex vivo* (cell-culture-based) tests for efficacy and toxicity, normally involving multiple rounds of testing, improvement, testing again, etc.

Many compounds will be discarded at this stage and many projects will be outright cancelled. It should be noted that, unlike academia, industry research is very focused on achieving something tangible and *saleable*. This means that research projects will be ruthlessly cut if they do not appear to be making progress or if the market conditions are no longer as tempting. The general approach taken by industry is that it is better to cut a program too early than to spend millions on clinical trials and then realise the mistake. The corollary of this, unfortunately, is that you should expect at least one project to be cancelled at some stage during your career. Yes, it will suck. Yes, you will get over it.

Compounds which make it through this gauntlet, known as **lead compounds**, will be ready for animal studies, known as **pre-clinical testing**. Drugs normally need to be tested on mice and another model species (which acts as a surrogate for the disease) prior to going into human trials. Animal studies normally focus on the metabolism and trafficking of the drug throughout the body to help determine target dosages, dosing frequency, etc. The other side of animal studies lies in identifying the toxicity caused by the treatment – both single doses and continuous treatment. Almost every drug on the market will cause toxic effects to some degree, the important thing is to know *when* and *how* this happens. Information at this stage will be used to decide (a) if the drug should go into human testing and (b) if so, what the dosage should be.

All of this information is gathered together and used by regulatory affairs to write the application for an Investigational New Drug (IND) or Clinical Trial Application (CTA), respectively the US or EU requirement to begin clinical trials. Other countries will have other requirements for beginning clinical trials, but the majority of pharmaceutical companies begin with the two largest markets first. If the regulatory authorities agree that the data gathered so far support the drugs' safety and efficacy, then it will be approved for further testing and will move to the next step.

Clinical trials

To get a drug approved for sale you must show that it is safe and effective in humans. How do you do this? Well, this is where clinical trials come in – planned and heavily regulated tests of new therapeutics. Clinical trials are divided into **Phases**, ranging from Phase I through to Phase IV, with each subsequent phase being larger and more expensive than the previous one.

The different phases of the clinical trial process

Clinical Phase	Patient numbers	Study duration	Purpose of study	Progression to next stage
Phase I	20-100	Months	Safety and dosage	70%
Phase II	Up to several hundred	Months – years	Efficacy and side effects	30-35%
Phase III	300 – 3000	Several years	Efficacy and side effects	25-30%
Phase IV	Several thousand	Variable	Safety and efficacy	n.a.

Phase I trials are safety trials, most often conducted using healthy volunteers rather than those actually suffering from the disease. They are designed to check what side effects are associated with the drug under investigation. More properly known as **adverse events**, every drug will cause a number of side effects – Phase I trials help to determine what they are and whether they are dangerous. The trials also study **ADME** (absorption, distribution, metabolism, and excretion) – essentially how the drug is taken up by the body, shuttled around from organ to organ, broken down into other compounds, and gotten rid of. This information is combined with ascending dose studies, in which the dosage of therapeutic is slowly increased over time to determine the point at which safety concerns occur. This helps to determine what the most likely therapeutic dosage should be in later work. The majority of small biotech firms will have a compound or two in Phase I trials.

Phase II trials begin to focus on efficacy, taking place in actual patients rather than the healthy volunteers of Phase I. The numbers involved are still quite small, usually less than a few hundred, and will often involve multiple **treatment arms** in which patients are given different dosing regimens to see which is the most effective. Phase II is usually too small to state whether a drug is definitely beneficial or not, but it provides the scientific data which the later studies will build from. Successfully passing Phase II will provide the first major boost to a biotech start-up and is usually the trigger for another round of investment.

Phase III is the big trial, often known as the pivotal study. They involve hundreds to thousands of patients spread across many different medical centres, all undertaking many tests and providing vast amounts of data for statistical analysis. Their size provides an excellent overview of potential safety issues, in particular long-term or rare effects, and so are carefully examined by regulatory authorities. The size and duration of these studies comes with a correspondingly high price tag. Due to their expense, Phase III trials are reserved for a pharmaceutical company's best prospects – although despite this compounds will often fail to meet the defined **clinical endpoint** and have thus managed to sink many a company's dreams. Medicines which are being developed for several different indications (i.e. several different diseases) will need to run a Phase III trial for each indication – with the same price tag as before.

Lastly there are **Phase IV** clinical trials which occur after the pharmaceutical has received approval. These are performed to answer remaining questions about efficacy or safety, and so can be extremely large trials over a long period of time. These are very often a requirement for drugs which have been approved via an accelerated pathway (those which address an urgent or unmet need for treatment) to demonstrate that there are no underlying safety issues.

Regulatory approval

Regulatory affairs will be involved in processes throughout the entire lifetime of the drug, from development through to post-approval lifecycle management. Their role is to act as the intermediary between the company and regulatory authorities such as the FDA. This section will provide an overview of the regulatory tasks involved, though those interested in the field may want to read our other publications (pg. 122).

Involvement by regulatory affairs really takes off once the drug has completed pre-clinical testing and is considered ready for clinical trials. Before any new compound can be tested on humans, the company requires permission from the **regulatory health authority** (e.g. the FDA) to conduct clinical trials. The application to get this permission is known as an Investigational New Drug Application in the US and a Clinical Trial Application in the EU. The application will be a large, complicated document containing information covering the manufacturing process, animal pharmacology/toxicology studies, and detailed plans for proposed clinical trials. Once the agency has had time to review the application and no questions have come up, the company is given the ok to move on to clinical testing.

Meetings with the authorities are more frequent during clinical trial stages than during preclinical development, and as the clinical trials proceed regulatory will be involved in sharing information between everyone involved. While **efficacy** can usually only be shown at the *end* of each clinical trial (unless the drug is much better than expected), **safety** problems can occur at any time (and the authorities will be very interested in safety problems). Because of this a typical clinical update will often be mostly comprised of tables and tables of adverse events which have occurred, their severity, and whether they were drug-related or not.

Compounds which are successful in clinical trials (Phase III in particular) will be ready for the big step, that of writing the initial dossier. This is known as writing the New Drug Application (NDA) in the US or the Marketing Authorisation Application (MAA) in the EU and it is *the* application, the one which will allow you to sell your drug. As such it has to be perfect. Regulatory managers will be under a lot of stress as they bring all of the data together and so will enjoy long days and very little free time at this point. The writing process itself can stretch for over a year and will involve sifting through reports, pulling information out and including in the dossier in a way that is honest but persuasive.

Submitting these applications will result in the health authority coming back with **Requests for Information** (RfIs) – i.e. the health authority in question isn't happy with something and would like to get some more information. Every submission will trigger RfIs of some form or another, and the time you have to respond to them can vary from indefinite through to a week or two. RfIs can be thought of as the regulatory version of reviewer comments after submitting an academic publication: some will be sensible suggestions, some will be stupid ideas, and some will take too long to do. As with reviewer comments, each will need to be replied to with a well-thought-out justification regarding your change, response, or lack thereof.

Finally, once the dossier has been sent off and approval gained, the new pharmaceutical is ready to be sold on the market. The work of regulatory affairs is not yet done, however, as there will now be a number of 'lifecycle management' activities taking up their time. This includes the preparation of annual reports (yearly updates regarding your product which are sent to the health authorities) and change evaluation – determining the regulatory requirements of proposed process changes (see pg. 27).

Audits and Inspections

If there was ever a word to strike fear into the hearts of employees everywhere, it is 'audit'. An audit is a systematic and tenacious investigation into processes and records at a facility such as a pharmaceutical manufacturing line. Audits are regularly conducted by health authorities to verify that the pharmaceutical is being developed or manufactured according to GxP (this is usually known as an inspection), and will occur before the drug is approved and then regularly afterwards. An international manufacturing centre with multiple products sold around the world will often have an audit from a different country every few weeks. Audits are also performed internally within the company (to find problems before the health authorities do) and by the company on other companies (to ensure that suppliers are up to scratch). Although audits and inspections will end up involving employees from numerous branches, the main department involved will be those from the quality assurance groups.

External inspections (from, say, the FDA) will usually last one to two weeks and will have a number of 'scope' items – these are the areas which the inspection wants to pay particular attention to. The inspectors will do a tour of the facilities, asking questions about processes and what people do when this or that occurs. They will take over a boardroom and ask to see documents and hear explanations from employees regarding potential issues. Documents and experts will be searched out and prepared by the 'back office', a nearby room full of stressed employees whose job is to figure out what the inspectors want to see and then show it to them – preferably without glaring holes in the data. As you can imagine this is an extremely stressful time for all involved, and will generally involve putting all other work on hold for the duration.

Once the inspection is complete the inspectors will provide verbal observations (the 'unofficial' version) and written observations (the very official version, often posted online for all to see). Generally a company will be expected to fix all issues which were identified during an inspection and then provide a response showing what they are doing to resolve the problems. The back-office will normally identify a number of problems while preparing for the audit, thus even a successful inspection will lead to a number of **Corrective and Preventative Actions** (CAPAs) and requirements for process improvement.

Production

Once a drug has exited the initial screening phases and becomes an actual pipeline molecule, the big question becomes 'how will we make it?' Small biotech start-ups will usually outsource production to contract manufacturers, large pharma firms will have their own manufacturing facilities. This can be a simple and well-established process (small molecule generics such as aspirin, for example), or it can be highly complex with many variables to tweak (as is the case for almost all biologicals, which require numerous purification steps after protein expression). All production will need to be done under **Good Manufacturing Practice** (GMP), essentially a set of common requirements for making high-quality goods.

There are two parts to any pharmaceutical. The first and most important of these is known as the **active pharmaceutical ingredient** (API) – this is the part that actually does something. It can be a small molecule like aspirin, it can be a large cancer-targeting antibody, it can be a strand of therapeutic DNA – regardless of what it is, the action of the drug is *due to the API*. The second part consists of the **excipients**, literally everything in the finished product that is not the API. This covers things such as bulking agents (to make the tablet easier to see), stability enhancers (to stop your drug degrading), preservatives, etc. etc. Excipients are extremely important for making the drug work as it should and so are a major component of the development process.

The production process can be thought of as a number of **process steps** linked together, each step indicating a single action in the manufacturing line such as mixing compounds, filter-sterilising, etc. Scattered amongst the process steps will be tests designed to monitor the overall progression of the process and the quality of the intermediate material being produced. These tests and measurements are known as **in-process controls** and **process parameters** respectively, and the manner in which they fit together can be somewhat complex.

As mentioned, there is a set process for taking the raw materials and converting them into a final product. The intermediate stages and materials will have a number of **quality attributes** (QAs), which are the properties or characteristics which affect the final product. These attributes are affected by variations in the process parameters (PPs), the term for measurable variables which occur during manufacturing. These process parameters are then monitored by in-process controls (IPCs), which are the measurements and values that will be taken as the process continues.

Here is a simple example process: the dossier describes the mixing of the Active Pharmaceutical Ingredient, with two secondary, non-active excipients in a buffer. The homogeneity of the final mixture would be a *quality attribute* – itself reliant on the *process parameter* of mixing time – while the act of measuring the mixing time would be an *in-process control*. The length of time that the mixing should occur is a target value, specification, or requirement.

IPCs, PPs, and attributes are divided up according to their criticality (how much of an effect they will have on the final product's quality and safety), splitting them into the categories Critical, Key and Non-key. As a general rule, all of these IPCs and PPs will be listed in the master batch record (the step-by-step checklist that you work through to make the final drug) but only a subset of these will be part of the regulatory application.

Multiple batches of drug product will be produced in a single **manufacturing campaign**, after which the line is often changed over to another product or strength. As each batch is finished it is packaged and labelled, then passed on to the quality group for batch release.

Deviations and CAPAs

At some point in the process, something will go wrong. What actually goes wrong and the severity of that problem can vary immensely, but something will inevitably go wrong.

Most problems during production will occur when a measured value, used to monitor the process, falls outside the expected range. As we mentioned in the previous section, there are several sets of ranges used in production. Values can vary enough that they fall outside the set **alert levels** (at which point we need to sit up and take notice), outside the set **action limits** (where we have to act to fix the problem), or outside the **acceptance limits** (at which our product is no longer acceptable).

A general term for these larger mistakes is a **deviation**, these often occur when someone does something which is not according to the plan – the drug substance isn't thawed correctly, the autoclave sterilisation cycle is wrong, documents weren't stored in the right place, an SOP wasn't followed, etc. etc. Deviations will be investigated by **quality assurance** (QA), whose job is to look at what happened and determine why. Why it happened, why the circumstances for it to happen were there, why those circumstances occurred – QA's ultimate goal is to determine the underlying reason for the deviation, known as the **root cause**. Sometimes this simply cannot be determined, so the investigation will have to stick to the more superficial reasons behind the problem – this is obviously not ideal but occurs quite often.

Once the root cause has been identified (if it can be), solutions to the problems need to be identified. These are known as **CAPAs** (corrective and preventative actions) and are defined actions which need to be taken in order to prevent the deviation occurring again. A simple and very common CAPA is simply to increase the amount of training which operators receive but you will also often see CAPAs asking for further studies or changes to current SOPs.

Once the root cause has been assigned and CAPAs created, it's time for QA to write up the deviation report. This report is basically a description of what went wrong, why it went wrong, and what's being done to fix it (more complicated than that, naturally, but that's the basics). This report is signed, put on file, and the deviation is considered 'closed'. Only when all the deviations associated with a batch have been closed can it be considered ready to move to the next step.

Batch release

Although manufacturing may be complete, a batch of drug substance or drug product cannot be **released** to the next stage until everyone is satisfied that the quality of the batch is acceptable. This means that the batch must meet **release specifications** during testing and have no associated open deviations. Testing and release are the respective domains of quality control and quality assurance groups, and both of these sides must be satisfied before the batch can be shipped off for sale.

So, what are specifications then? Specifications are the properties which a batch of something, be it a raw material or finished product, needs to have in order to be considered acceptably well-made. Each specification has an associated testing method, an analytical test which determines the value of that property. A simple example would be a visual control, an 'analytical method' which basically involves just looking at the sample – a sample specification sheet for sucrose would then state *'visual control: white powder'*. Although basic, visual controls are a common testing method because of their simplicity and almost negligible costs. Naturally there are more complex analytical methods and associated specifications: materials may need to match defined infrared spectra, chromatographic techniques may be used to show impurity levels, the number of bacteria present in the product needs to be determined, the pH range has to be confirmed, etc. etc.

The method used to test a specification is often provided in a **pharmacopeia**, a hefty publication produced by organisations in many of the larger countries which will specify how exactly you should go about testing things. The most important ones are those published by the European Union (known as Ph. Eur.) and the United States (known as USP), but others are produced by Japan, Britain, etc. The method described in the pharmacopeia is usually considered 'best practice' by the country concerned – this makes it very hard to convince a regulatory authority a *non*-pharmacopeia method is an acceptable substitute. Because of this, almost all pharmaceutical companies will try to ensure that their methods comply with at least one of USP or Ph. Eur.

Some products and raw materials, particularly common ones, will also have **monographs** in the pharmacopeia. A monograph will describe the typical specifications and tests which should be used to ensure that any particular product is of a good quality. Take aspirin, for example. The USP monograph for aspirin lists numerous specifications which should be achieved by pure aspirin. An example specification is listed as "*Residue on Ignition: not more than 0.05%*". The associated testing method is USP <281>, part of the US Pharmacopeia, and section 281 describes in detail just *how* you should burn your sample and see what is left over afterwards.

Not all pharmacopeia specifications are the same – Japan for example is notoriously tougher with their requirements than other countries. This means that a drug may be approved with different specifications in one country than another, and this in turn means that a batch may be acceptable for one country but not another. The batch release process will take this into account when deciding where the product can be shipped to. Once the batch of material has been shown to comply with the release specifications, it can be officially approved for release and thus either move on to production (in the case of raw materials and drug substance) or be shipped out to market (for the finished drug product).

Sales and marketing
As with every other product in the world, pharmaceuticals are marketed to customers. Unlike many other products, there are a number of regulations which cover just how pharmaceuticals can

be marketed – designed to prevent unscrupulous practices or patients being taken advantage of. As a rule the target customers for pharmaceutical marketing are health care professionals, not patients themselves. The two exceptions to this rule are the United States and New Zealand, both of which allow direct-to-consumer advertising of prescription drugs and so have numerous television advertisements for almost every condition imaginable.

Pharmaceuticals can be marketed to health care professionals in a number of ways. The stereotypical method that everyone has heard of is that of free samples – this is not just the labelled 'freebies' (notepads, stress-balls, USB keys, etc.) but also includes trial packs of medication. Industry groups will also sponsor **continuing medical education**, the seminars covering updated medical techniques which doctors are required to attend to keep their skills up to date. Marketing will also be involved in the production of scientific articles, online videos, social events for physicians, and trade show exhibitions.

Despite this, a large portion of pharmaceutical marketing is performed by pharmaceutical sales representatives, employees of the company whose role is to visit **prescribers** (those who can prescribe the drug) every couple of weeks. The area which a sales representative covers is determined by the number of prescribers present – a specialty medication will have fewer potential prescribers than a more general one and thus the sale representatives' area will be correspondingly larger. Physicians who write more prescriptions or are considered influential in the field will tend to have more visits than their less-important colleagues.

Highly influential physicians are known as **key opinion leaders (KOLs)**, and are usually heavily targeted by marketing efforts in an attempt to persuade them of the benefits of the pharmaceutical – the intention being that the KOL will then influence others. Sales representatives tend to be the largest component of a firms' marketing effort, with direct visits strongly affecting pharmaceutical sales. It also has a tendency to be the most problematic, with numerous legal actions having been triggered against pharmaceutical firms based on alleged **off-label** promotion by sales reps.

The other side of marketing is market access, which can be thought of as the negotiations required before someone (the government, companies) will actually *pay* for the pharmaceutical. Patients rarely pay for the entire cost of medication themselves, instead using public or private health insurance to spread the risks and costs over a large number of people. The company or government department offering this insurance determines the price which they will pay for the medication – this will come down to a number of factors including efficacy of the treatment, prevalence of the disease, and how serious the disease is.

The difficulty here lies in comparing the severity of different diseases. As an example, which is the more severe of these options: late-onset Alzheimer's disease, Down's syndrome, or complete blindness? To attempt to resolve these problems, a generalised measure known as the **quality-adjusted life-year** (QALY) was developed. In this system, a year of perfect health is considered to be 1 QALY and a year of being dead is 0, with various levels of disability in-between. QALY calculations allow those who pay for the medication to calculate whether the benefit it brings is worth the cost – as an example the UK has previously described a cost-effective medical intervention as being one costing less than GBP 20,000 per QALY. This is then the basis for a long, drawn-out negotiation between groups of people from the pharmaceutical company and health insurer, one which theoretically will lead to an acceptable price at the end of the day.

Follow-up stability
There's no point in making a fantastically high-quality drug if it falls apart a few weeks after you make it. All therapeutics thus need a respectable **shelf-life** – the length of time that the drug can sit on the shelf and still be of sufficient quality that it can be used. Shelf-life is determined throughout the development and scale-up

process and is predominantly related to results from **stability studies**.

Stability studies involve (essentially) taking a large number of product samples and then sticking them in a room somewhere. The room will have a controlled environment, with consistent temperature and humidity, and this is known as the study conditions – for example biological therapeutics are often stored in the fridge at 4°C and so the **intended study conditions** will have a temperature of 4°C (or, more realistically, 2-8°C). This simulates the actual aging product of the drug in storage and lets the developer see how it will degrade over time. Other 'defined' conditions exist to mimic room temperature storage, tropical climates, desert zones, etc.

As well as intended conditions, stability studies will also include **accelerated conditions** – these are intended to force the degradation of the product at a higher rate than would be seen under intended storage conditions. This allows degradation to be observed within a reasonable timeframe (rather than waiting for several years each time) and thus most applications to health authorities will include a full set of accelerated data, a portion of the intended condition data, and a commitment to provide the remaining information as it becomes available.

Standard stability testing zones

Condition	Mimics	Temperature Range	Humidity Range in relative humidity (%)
Zone I	Temperate zone	21°C ± 2°C	45% RH ± 5% RH
Zone II	Mediterranean/su btropical zone	25°C ± 2°C	60% RH ± 5% RH
Zone III	Hot, dry zone	30°C ± 2°C	35% RH ± 5% RH
Zone IV	Hot, humid/tropical zone	30°C ± 2°C	65% RH ± 5% RH

Refrigerated	The fridge	5°C ± 3°C	No Humidity
Frozen	The freezer	-15°C ± 5°C	No Humidity
Accelerated Ambient	Accelerated conditions for room-temperature	40°C ± 2°C	75% ± 5% RH
Accelerated Refrigerated	Accelerated conditions for refrigerated	25°C ± 2°C	60% ± 5% RH
Accelerated Frozen	Accelerated conditions for frozen	5°C ± 3°C	No Humidity
Intermediate	'Middle' accelerated, not often used	30°C ± 2°C	65% ± 5% RH

Each stability study has a number of **pull points**, which can be thought of as defined time points at which a number of the samples will be taken out of the climate-controlled room ('pulled') and tested. The dates of the pull points and the tests being performed are defined before the study begins in the study protocol, a very important document which describes everything that will be done throughout the entire two or three years. Once signed, the protocol *cannot be changed* without writing a formal amendment and signing this as well – this is intended to prevent people from 'accidentally' forgetting a couple of tests when they start to show unwanted results.

Pull point testing involves a number of analytical techniques, these differ from product to product but are all intended to show the overall quality. Measured values need to comply with **shelf-life specifications**, a slightly broader set of specifications which apply to products sitting on the shelf (as opposed to release specifications, which apply to the product just after manufacture). Both release and shelf-life specifications are a matter of negotiation between the company and the health authority during the regulatory approval process. Data from studies performed during the development and scale-up processes will be used to show how long the drug can be stored before problems occur – this then sets the shelf life.

Stability studies are required when developing a new product, when making large changes to the production process, or as part of the yearly follow-up-stability-testing (FUST), in which a single batch per year is placed into stability testing to ensure that everything is ok. As with all stability testing, FUST starts with a stability protocol and ends with a stability report detailing all of the results and trends. Due to their ubiquity it is very likely that those involved in the manufacturing side of pharmaceuticals will end up involved with (or just hearing about) stability studies. The studies themselves are usually conducted by QC or QA but will require input from other departments, particularly when the protocol and report documents are being finalised.

Change control
A major part of the post-approval product lifecycle is that of **change control**. A regulatory dossier can be considered as a contract between the company and the relevant health authority, stating that the drug will be manufactured *exactly* as is written in the dossier, no changes allowed. Processes, however, will always change over time – the people in production and development will think of better ways to make something, a supplier of plastic bottles will go bankrupt and thus require a replacement, the supplier stays the same but the plastic bottle manufacturing site will change… Each of these changes can and will occur.

Because process changes are inevitable, every pharmaceutical company has systems in place to identify, evaluate, and implement these changes – this is known as change control. This is a multi-step process: beginning with change *evaluation* (part of the planning stage), then *notification* (informing the health authority of your plan), next comes *approval* (assuming they like the plan, at least), then finally *implementation* (actually changing the process). Regulatory authorities call this post-approval notification and it is performed in different ways for different regions. In general, however, the process will depend on the severity of this change: approval can be instantaneous (make the change, notify later), require notification (either before or when making the change) or be a large enough change that nothing can be done before the authority gives the ok.

Prospective changes will be evaluated by multiple departments within the pharmaceutical company, the exact identity of which will vary based on what the change actually is. In general, however, quality assurance and regulatory affairs will be required to assess the majority of prospective changes. Their respective jobs are to indicate whether the change will affect product quality or approval status (and if it does, what sort of costs will be involved). From these evaluations, a group within the company will decide if the change should go ahead.

Pharmacovigilance

Pharmacovigilance is a vital part of ensuring that a drug is safe to use, being the process of detecting and identifying any adverse events which may be caused by a pharmaceutical. As well as **adverse events** from the patient (i.e. side-effects), pharmacovigilance will collect information on medication errors (e.g. overdoses, inappropriate use), failures in the packaging or application method (e.g. a broken needle in an auto-injector), or cases where the drug shows a lack of efficacy. This information is gathered from a number of sources, the most common of these being direct reports from patients and healthcare providers. Further sources include medical literature or internal reports (all employees of a pharmaceutical firm are required to report suspected adverse events to their respective pharmacovigilance group, for example).

Adverse events need to be reported to the relevant health authority, a requirement in almost every country. Each individual report needs to have an identifiable patient, reporter, drug, and adverse event, the reports are then rated based on how serious the adverse event is (anything requiring hospitalisation, for example, is automatically in the top category). Serious events must be reported to health authorities within 1-2 weeks (depending on the country), less serious events are bundled together into a weighty document known as the periodic safety update report (PSUR) or periodic benefit risk evaluation report (PBRER). This is sent to numerous countries around the world and provides a snapshot of all adverse events which have occurred in the last reporting period.

The point of all this paperwork, of course, is to make sure that drugs which are on the market do not suddenly start showing nasty side-effects. History has shown that many drugs end up being less safe than expected after approval. The most well-known of these is thalidomide (which caused horrible birth defects) but there have been numerous others such as anti-arthritic Vioxx (higher risk of heart attacks), anti-obesity treatment Fen-Phen (heart valve failure), or the cholesterol-reducing Baycol (muscle decay and subsequent death from kidney failure). Alongside these problems are manufacturing defects (e.g. Able Labs, whose entire product line-up had to be withdrawn due to quality control issues) and even deliberate sabotage (e.g. the poisoning of Tylenol capsules in 1982).

Because of the potential for harm governments are *very* interested in adverse events, thus most pharmaceutical companies will have a dedicated pharmacovigilance department with responsibility for adverse event reporting. This department will spend a lot of time investigating and aggregating reports, working closely with regulatory affairs and other departments during the preparation and submission of PSURs and other updates.

Starting out: getting through the first few months

Regardless of the position you have taken, the first few months of your new job will be a whirlwind of new people to meet, new things to learn, and new acronyms to puzzle out. Rather than feeling lost and confused, look at this as (a) a giant learning opportunity (which it is) and (b) a chance to get started on making your reputation as a valuable and professional employee. This section will cover the typical events and expectations which will occur during your first few months.

Before you start

You've signed the contract, you've gotten the info packet from HR, and you know when your first day will be. No worries, right? Wrong. This is the first step that you're taking into a completely different world, and it's really easy to start that step on the wrong foot. Before you even get to your first day you should plan out a few important things.

Have you organised the paperwork?

There will be a lot of paperwork involved in starting a new job. Large companies will have done a lot of it beforehand, smaller companies may wait until the day you arrive. In any case you are likely to need information regarding your bank account, tax details, work permit (if you're from overseas), current residence, superannuation/pension/401k details, qualifications – all of those little things you tend to forget about before the big day. Get in touch with HR before you start and ask what exactly they will need to see.

How are you going to get there?

Seems like a pretty obvious question, doesn't it? But you should know where the site or building will be. If it's a large site, are you being met at the gate? Which one? When? Are you driving to work? If so, do you know where you can park, how much it will cost? Have you remembered various value coins just in case it's one of *those* parking meters? Or are you taking public transport? In which case you should know the timetables, where you'll be getting on and off – and you should probably know the number of a taxi company just in case.

This planning is all in the aid of *not being late* on your first day, which is a very bad impression to give when starting out. If the area is completely unfamiliar to you, you might want to think about doing a practice run – try to travel to your new job at around the same time you would be on your first day. See how long it takes, whether there are traffic jams or complex routes you need to be aware of. The practice run will give you a better idea of conditions on your first day. If nothing else you can go grab a coffee afterwards and see what sort of food and drinks are in the neighbourhood.

What are you going to wear?
It seems a bit shallow, yes, but we are judged based on what we wear. Different companies have different policies, even different groups within the same company will dress completely differently. You should have met people from your new group or department during the interview process. How did they dress? What was said regarding dress-code during the interview? You want to be about that level, slightly fancier if possible. That doesn't mean that you should turn up in a suit and tie (if nothing else, people will assume that you're in upper management during the introduction talks) – it does mean that you should match what is expected from employees. Try not to slum it in track-pants and a singlet – the saying "dress for the job you want" is a cliché but holds true, you'll get more respect in a shirt (or at least a polo) than a t-shirt. If you don't have an appropriate wardrobe, now is the time to go shopping!

The First Day

First day of the new job! Most large pharmaceutical companies will have the first 1-2 days involve some sort of 'onboarding' or introduction program, assuming that you're turning up in line with a normal intake cycle. People starting at odd times may go directly into the office with an introduction program to follow. Regardless of which one you will be following, the first day is really about introducing yourself to people and beginning to get yourself organised. No-one expects that you will do anything useful, so use the time available to get ready for the upcoming weeks.

By the end of your first day, you should know:

- The names and faces of the people on your team, and have at least a reasonable chance of matching the two together.
- Who your boss is.
- Where your desk is or will be.
- A good idea of the typical working hours – are you expected to be in early, do most people start late, etc.
- Where the nearest fire extinguisher and emergency exit is (seems boring, but you'll regret not knowing if it ever becomes an issue).

Although you aren't expected to be competent, your new colleagues *will* be judging you based on how you act and how you communicate. Start the new job off on a high note, and try to remember a few important things:

Get there early

It looks really bad when you turn up late on your first day. So don't. You want to be there around 10-15 minutes before your official start time. This is enough buffer time to prevent minor problems making you late, but not so much that you'll be the weirdo haunting the lobby scaring the security guard.

Dress appropriately

It's your first day, and (realistically) everyone is going to be making some sort of snap judgement about your competence and likeability. They shouldn't. But yeah, they will. So the first step is to dress well, especially on the first day – dress a little bit better than the other people that will be around. If it's a shirt and nice pants job, then wear a suit. T-shirt and pants, wear a shirt and pants. You don't want to be over-dressed, but aim to look just a little bit better than you'd normally manage.

Say hi

Just say hello. The best way to make a good first impression is to be friendly and confident, and just saying hello is an excellent way to give off that vibe. You'll get the usual questions right after that – where are you from? What will you be doing? Why did you decide to work here? You may as well think about what you'll say here, because these questions are bound to come up. Don't forget to ask questions of the people you meet too. You'll be working with them for a while and a friendly conversation or two will go a long way.

The first two weeks

You've gotten past the basic information that comes in the first day, so now's the time to start planning for the longer term. Industry has a very different set of priorities compared to academia – you will be expected to focus on the team projects and tasks rather than going off on your own tangent. This also means that they will want you to be somewhat self-reliant with at least a vague idea of what you are doing within the first two weeks.

After the first two weeks in your new role you should be able to answer several questions:

- What are your responsibilities in this position?
- What are your goals? How will you (and the company) know they have been achieved?
- What's a typical career path from where you are now? How long will it take you to move upwards?
- How is the company structured and who will be telling you what to do? (In particular, who is your boss? And their boss?)

- How do all of the HR things such as leave, holidays and insurance work? On which day will you be paid, and how often?
- Where do you get all your computer programs, stationary, office furniture and the like?
- How do you track your time worked?

There's so much to learn!

You want to be effective at your job, naturally, and this requires learning a lot of things in a short period of time. Not only how to do your work, but also who your contacts are within the company, how the internal systems and programs work, which meetings you need to attend – even things as mundane as where you can find the pens. Almost all of this information will be dumped on you within the first week or two, usually starting on your first day in the new position. So how do you keep on top of it all?

Read up beforehand

You'll need to know the background behind the company you're working for. I don't mean all of the history of its foundation as a dye factory back in the 1800s (as so many pharmaceutical companies were). Instead you should know the answers to the important questions: what sort of products does the firm make? Where do they derive most of their income? What are they focusing on? Big pharma tends to have large pipelines with a couple of blockbusters, small biotech companies will focus on one or two core products. This kind of information is easily found on the company website or through web searches – and there's no excuse *not* to know it.

Ask questions

Some people say that there is no such thing as a dumb question. This is unfortunately not true most of the time. At the very start of a new job, however, you can ask the most ridiculous things you want and people *will still answer them*. Use this grace period to get answers to things you want to know, within limits. Your first approach should be trying to find the answer online or via any helpful materials the company has provided. If it's easily answered in that time then you would just annoy people by asking. If it takes longer than 5-10 minutes, however, then go ask your question! At this point it's far more efficient to ask for help than to waste time.

Who do you ask? Generally you will be assigned to a more experienced worker whose job is to get you up to speed, some larger companies even make this a formal process. They should be your first port of call, try to organise a time where you can sit down with a coffee and run through a list of questions – what does this mean? What's this acronym? Why do we do this? Ask whatever you want here, their job is to answer your questions.

Take notes, be organised
If you don't write it down, you'll forget it. Simple as that. There's so much new information that sticking it all into your brain and hoping it stays is being optimistically stupid. Carry a notebook around with you to all of those early meetings and training sessions. When you hear or read something which will be relevant to you or your job, write it down. We'll cover note-taking and keeping notes organised later, but for now the important thing is to remember to *write it down*.

Your company style
Every large firm and most of the smaller ones will have a typical 'style' in how they put everything together. This may involve using a set of colours for presentations, there may be a set template which needs to be filled in for some reports, possibly even dedicated add-ins for Word or PowerPoint to keep everything looking consistent. The important thing is that you should match and understand this style in the work you do. Get the hang of the fonts and colours used, learn to use the templates or add-ins. You will be writing a lot in the future, now's the time to get the hang of it.

The first two months

After two months you should be settling into the new role, you've done all the introduction rounds, know all the faces around you (if not the names) and you are building up some confidence in the work you are able to do. You should be able to do the following things without too much hesitation:

- Be able to perform simple tasks in your field without needing your hand held.
- Understand what the different departments in the company actually do and how they relate to each other.
- Be able to use the most important IT systems which relate to your job.
- Understand the most typical documents which you will work with.
- Have a grasp of any regulatory rules which affect your field.

The most of important of these, of course, is being able to do your job. Almost every company will expect you to be working on actual useful things by this stage – you will still be heavily supervised by either your manager or your assigned mentor but you should understand the basics well enough to be doing your designated job. Having said this, never be afraid to speak to your manager if you feel that something is too complex or too important for you to make a decision on – the overconfident newbie ruining everything because they never asked questions is a stereotype for a reason. Ask questions when in doubt!

Beyond this you should have a good grasp of the IT tools and regulatory rules which will cover the majority of your work.

Typical IT systems

Pharmaceutical firms are, in theory at least, at the cutting edge of technology – constantly pushing against the boundaries of what we know in order to bring novel, more effective, or cheaper medicines to the general public. Unfortunately many of them are large multinational companies, which means that the software you will end up using is likely to be at least 3-5 years old and will be designed with a complete indifference to usability. Frustrated at the latest bug in the system? Can't understand why the most useful function is hidden behind six different menu options? Take a deep breath. That's just how it is. There are a number of regulatory rules surrounding pharmaceutical-related software (covering things such as traceability and archiving, for example) and this in turn requires very careful development and debugging of software before it can be implemented. A crash on your home computer will be annoying (assuming you've backed up, at least), a crash on a pharma firm system will lose millions of dollars in lost productivity – avoiding this kind of disaster is the underlying reason for slow software updates.

There are several broad categories of software which will be present in almost every pharmaceutical firm. There will be databases full of information on batches which have been produced, their compliance to specifications, which countries they can be sold to, regulatory or QA issues, etc. There will be a document control system which allows multiple people to work on documents such as regulatory dossiers or QA reports (sometimes simultaneously) – this will usually be combined with some sort of approval and finalisation set-up to archive 'complete' versions. There will be some form of system which covers change control – the process by which changes to the current processes are evaluated and approved or rejected. Marketing and sales people will have access to a customer-relationship database system to help keep track of who buys what and how they can be persuaded to buy more. Laboratory groups will work with computerised laboratory-management/lab-book software. And so on.

It is very unlikely that you will have need of or even access to all of the software which is available in your company. You should, however, learn how to use the ones which make up your daily life. Spend a while going through menus and playing around with options – you will very often find that there are hidden shortcuts and methods which will make your working life much easier.

Regulatory rules

The pharmaceutical industry is threaded through with a multitude of regulations and regulatory bodies seeking to control the safety and efficacy of what is being produced. These are far too complex to cover in detail here (though those interested should see our other publications on pg. 122), so we will cover the 'main' regulatory areas: marketing approval, good manufacturing practice, and patenting. Your exact role in the industry will determine the regulations which you are most often in contact with, but everyone should have at least a passing knowledge of these main areas within the first two months of employment.

First, a drug needs to have **marketing approval** from the regulatory authority before it can be sold in a country. This means that the responsible government department (such as the FDA) has looked at your drug in detail and decided that is reliable enough to be sold. This is dependent on your preclinical and clinical results as well as your defined production process. Importantly, marketing approval is given for specific indications – a certain disease, type of cancer etc. A drug being used for a non-approved indication is known as **off-label** use. Off-label use is commonly performed by medical professionals who want to use another option for a difficult-to-treat disease, particularly when using generic drugs. However you as a pharmaceutical employee should *never* inform doctors of off-label uses for your drugs – this is very illegal, leading to fines and possibly criminal prosecution.

Second, all drugs need to be produced under what is known as **Good Manufacturing Practice**, or GMP. This internationally-shared set of guidelines is expanded upon by health authorities in each country, with the intention of ensuring that all drugs are made to the correct level of safety and efficacy. In practice this includes requirements such as keeping the facility clean and hygienic; clearly defining and documenting all of the manufacturing process steps; validating processes and changes as necessary; training everyone to do their tasks correctly; investigating when things go wrong; and (most importantly) keeping lots and lots of documents as you go along. You will hear a lot about GMP and the associated Good 'x' Practice (GxP) systems during your time in industry as it underlies almost everything that we do.

Lastly, the existence of **patents** heavily affects how a drug is developed. Patents provide an exclusive right to the inventor to use an invention (a new drug, a new process, etc.) in exchange for the idea returning to the public domain after a set period of time. Although the idea is simple patenting in practice is a minefield of complexity. Patents can be filed for multiple overlapping ideas or extensions to the original idea, the fact that a patent is filed per-country rather than globally means a drug may be protected in one land but not the neighbouring one, etc. Complicating this is the notion of **exclusivity**, in which health authorities prevent competing drugs from reaching the market for a set period of time based on the type of new drug being approved. Thus the granting of a patent is only the first step in a long process, and indeed almost every patent with value will be fought over by patent attorneys at some stage.

Impressing colleagues: Be great at your job

The road to success and a good career is a fairly simple one at this stage – be great at your job. Not just good, because all companies expect you to be good, but great. What does this actually mean? You need to exceed expectations. You need to be better than a new employee, freshly arrived in industry, would normally be. How do you do that? Here are some tips:

Be independent

A lot of the larger pharmaceutical companies have specialised introduction programs where they'll talk about the company and some of its systems, they'll assign someone to you to answer your questions, they'll organise training for important software. When it happens it is fantastic – you should take advantage of every moment (i.e. actually pay attention and write notes). But the training won't cover everything and many smaller firms will have a shorter or non-existent introduction process. This is where *you* come in, because you have to be willing to learn how to do things yourself. Ask people for help, puzzle over things for a while, look up information online, and read over documents in your company intranet. With a science background you should be used to solving problems, so get those problem-solving skills to work on the job you've just been hired for.

Be professional

Yep, professional. Because you're a professional now. That means you have to act in a professional way, even when it's a terrible day. The best way to impress people is to be the calm one, even when everything is collapsing around you – be chilled, look positive, be polite, do your work. Easy? No, not at all, especially when the day starts with a random deviation in production while someone in QA realises that we've been doing everything wrong for three years and oh my god the FDA is going to come down on us like a tonne of bricks... Chaos. This will happen far more often that you would expect, so be prepared for these moments to happen. Stay calm, breathe deeply, and solve the problem. Then repeat.

Having said that, sometimes everything really is too much, especially if you also have problems at home or outside the work environment. If you are at the point where you are simply overwhelmed with the job, just stop for a moment. Take half an hour, preferably outside the office, to grab a coffee or a drink and calm down (don't go to the pub, trust me on this). Once you're back to being calm, then come back and resume work where you left it. Half an hour away from the desk won't make a huge difference in the grand scheme of things and the break will help you immensely.

As in all jobs, everyone will instantly look you up on social media once you begin to see just what sort of person you are. And the person you are should *appear* to be a professional one. Clean up your profile, lock it down, doesn't matter – just make sure HR can't see your drinking marathon from the weekend. Similarly, don't get wasted at the social event or Christmas party. Free drinks are great, people spending the next few weeks talking about how you spent the night falling over less so. This also applies to those times that you attend a business lunch or dinner. Be professional – don't order the most expensive thing there, don't start until everyone has their food, don't spit food on the people you're trying to sell stuff to. Easy, right?

Be patient
It's a completely new world, especially if you're jumping across from academia directly. Nobody really cares that you had a whole bunch of really great publications, nobody thinks that your years of discussions with professors will bring great insights to the company. You've been hired based on your cleverness, your ability to learn, and your ability to solve problems. Don't expect to be given high level responsibilities at the start, don't expect to *understand* everything at the start. Instead, you need to be patient. Learn as much as you can, but recognise that it will take time. Do the boring, pointless jobs you get handed. But do them well, and

aim to do them better than could be expected. Everyone starts at the bottom, the way you deal with these early tasks will determine whether you're trusted to do more complex work.

As you do it, keep notes for yourself: how to do it, how it could be done better, where would you improve the process? This kind of information is not only useful for you when you get stuck with the job a second time, but also helps others who need to do the same task. Cynical as it sounds, nothing will impress your co-workers as much as when you make their lives easier.

Basically – you're starting at the bottom. That's ok. Do the work you've been asked to do, accept that it will take time to learn enough that you're trusted with more interesting work. But plan your future career to build off the great work you do at the start.

Be open

The majority of people you'll end up working with are actually really nice. There's always an idiot or two, but on the whole you'll be surprised at the friendliness in the normally cut-throat world of pharmaceutical development. So don't spend your time complaining about that one person who everyone hates. Get out there, talk to people and make friends – ask about their lives, talk about your own. You'll spend a significant portion of your life at work, so it helps to actually *get along with* the people you'll see there.

Be polite

Being polite is pretty easy when it comes to conversations – don't interrupt people, listen more than you speak, pay attention to others. Being polite in an office environment can be more difficult for those used to a lab, but it all comes down to taking responsibility for problems, even if it isn't 'your fault'. What does this mean? If something's run out or broken, deal with it – put paper into the printer, tell someone that the plate reader is broken, order new supplies when you need to, or at least pass on the knowledge to people who do the ordering. And refill the coffee pot when you take the last cup (yes, you! Refill it).

Be knowledgeable

You're smart, right? Use it! Try to learn about your trade and your field – what are the big topics at the moment and how might they affect your company? What are the sort of problems and opportunities coming up for your little biotech firm or global pharma? There are a vast number of websites, magazines and podcasts out there which cover the pharmaceutical industry and which you can use to keep up to date – generally this is a great way to fill up your commuting time to work with something that doesn't require too much thought but is also helpful for your career. Career? Yes, managers are always impressed by people who know the bigger picture of the industry.

This naturally applies to your job as well. Learn what you are meant to be doing, understand the projects that you are involved in – this also includes the parts which are not directly related to your position. A broad knowledge of what everyone is doing will help you immensely in your day-to-day work, if only so you know who to call when something goes wrong. Having said that – don't be afraid to say 'I don't know'. Don't make up answers. You should, however, follow 'I don't know' with 'but I'll find out and let you know'. You're new, no-one knows everything, no problem there – you'll be saying 'I don't know' throughout your career. The important thing is to show that you are happy to find out, that's the part that really impresses people.

Be early

When you work is very different between companies – some places everyone gets in before 8am, some places are dead until 9 or 10am. Try to match those hours. Unlike a PhD where you can work whenever you want, so long as the job gets done, most industry jobs will have core times where everyone is expected to be there. This is mostly because of the extra meeting load, you need to be around when everyone else is to get to all those collaboration meetings and information exchange meetings and planning meetings and pre-meeting meetings (there are a *lot* of meetings). Industry jobs are about working with other people, you have to be there when they are.

From a purely career-oriented point of view you also want to try and get in a *little* bit before everyone else does. Turn up later than everyone else, even by only 15 minutes, and you'll be thought a bit of a slacker. If you're always there before the majority though, suddenly you're a go-getter with a career focus. Not fair? No, but that's how people are.

Be impressive

I'm already impressive! Well, you could be more impressive. Professionally impressive. Best way to achieve this? Always do everything a little bit better than people expected it to be. Quicker, more detail, nicer formatting – anything goes when you want to jazz up the stability report you were asked to get signed by yesterday. Remember that impressing your colleagues is a slow process with lots of little steps, built on many minor successes. Be patient, keep the good work coming. People *will* notice and your career *will* take off.

Managing upwards: Dealing with your boss

The starting phase of your career in pharma is heavily dependent on your relationship with your colleagues, most importantly on your relationship with your boss. This isn't as easy as you would think and will take a bit of effort on your behalf.

The important thing to remember is that you're new. Your boss doesn't really know you and you don't really know them. You may have completely different communications styles, they may never have had formal training in how to manage people, and they are certain to be much, much busier than you are. Because of this, it can sometimes be difficult to have a good working relationship from the start. You might not understand what they're after, or may think that they have no idea what they're doing. Be careful with this thought. Most people who reach management positions are likely to be both knowledgeable and successful – they have a lot that they could teach you and a lot that you can use to further your career. Building the working relationship you need, however, is very much up to you.

So be realistic and efficient. Your manager has limited time and so you must make the most of the meetings you do have with them. The wide range of personality types that are out there means that there's a good chance you won't click with your manager (or even like them, in some cases). The thing is – you're going to have to work well with all of them, regardless of time constraints, regardless of personalities. How do you manage this? You need to keep in mind the things which your manager will require – information, communication, and reliability. Keep them up-to-date wherever possible through things such as your one-on-one meeting and your weekly update. Take responsibility for your own work and your own decisions. Work well, and quickly.

The one-to-one meeting

You'll most likely be having one-to-one meetings alone with your boss every week or every second week. This is not a bad thing!

Your bosses' job is to keep you on track and help you get your projects done. Why? Because, like all managers, his success is directly linked to the success of the people he is managing (this, incidentally, is also something you need to keep in mind as you move up the corporate ladder). By meeting with you, alone, every week, your boss will be able to keep track of your progress and help you get used to the strange world that is the pharmaceutical industry.

Given that you'll have to have these meetings regardless of your desires, how can you make them useful and valuable to all concerned? The main answer here is quite simple: be organised, and don't waste time. You have too many projects going on, your boss has too many projects going on (and too many people to take care of) – neither of you can afford to waste time. So, just as with every other meeting you attend, you need to be organised before you get there.

Before you start, write yourself a list of topics that you want to discuss. This can be your latest progress on a task, it can be problems you've had, it can be questions about whether your project is about to be cancelled due to failing Phase III trials. It doesn't matter what it is, the idea is simply to get those topics down in a solid form where you can refer to them during the meeting. Now put them in order of importance – start with the topics which will have the most impact on your week (or life), work your way down to those of lesser importance. This is now your 'agenda' for the one-to-one.

Depending on your level of organisation, you can pass this agenda on to your manager before the meeting. Or you can just turn up with it – this is very much dependent on how formal your meetings tend to be. In either case you should aim to work through the list of topics, one after another, throughout the course of the meeting. Your boss will also have their own list of things to talk about, possibly overlapping yours, possibly not. Take turns to work through one item after another. This is not only faster than aimlessly wandering between conversation points but will also seriously impress your manager – they are rarely used to such organised one-on-ones.

Take notes during the meeting! It's very tempting to think that you can remember everything which is said, but this is completely wrong. You'll forget. They'll forget. Both of you will forget until one of those horrible Thursday mornings when you realise that the data for the annual report is due in one week and you haven't even started. Or worse, *you* will forget and that Thursday morning will consist of your manager asking how the data-gathering is going. Don't let yourself get into this situation. Take notes! More specifically, take notes of the important information you've been given. Record timelines and deadlines, project updates and their response to your project updates, tasks that you'll need to do and tasks which you should remind one of your co-workers about, because your manager forgot to do it in their one-on-one. Once you get out of the meeting, or at least within the next 24 hours, you'll want to move those notes into a readable and usable form – writing down tasks which need to be done, adding due dates to the calendar, recording general info for later. This helps you keep on top of all the work you tend to get assigned during the meeting, and ensures that you'll avoid being blindsided by a forgotten task later on. See pg. 60 for more information on note-taking.

Topics you should discuss
We've talked about how you should run the meeting with your manager, but what should you actually discuss? Obviously this will depend on which department you end up in – QA won't often discuss regulatory dossiers, for example, but there are a few things that you should focus on first regardless of your department.

First, what you are doing:
Particularly your progress on any tasks that were assigned by your manager (if you've finished any of them, now's the time to boast).

Second, problems which have come up:
Talk about the emergencies first but try to mention things before they become emergencies. If you have a problem, bring a couple

of suggestions for solving the problem with you – they may be complete rubbish, but at least you can both work from there to find an actual solution.

Third, advice and opinions:
Once the problems are out of the way then it's time to ask for advice on issues which will be important in the future.

Lastly, suggestions for current or future projects:
You've been hired for your brain, so use it. Just use it well – be very careful making arrogantly 'brilliant' suggestions a few weeks after you've started, just in case it is something that everyone with a bit of experience can see is a stupid idea.

Write a weekly update email

Your boss has a team of people that he needs to co-ordinate, more tasks than you can imagine, and far too many meetings. Ideally you'll be meeting every week for a 1:1, but this is often one of those ideals which doesn't quite work out. If you want to make them truly happy, you'll get into the habit of doing *proactive* progress updates. In other words, instead of them coming to ask what's going on, you let them know first – this is the sort of thing that makes managers very happy indeed.

How do you do this? An excellent way to keep your boss updated is by sending them a weekly email, usually on a Friday, as part of your own close-out/summary process (see pg. 71). What should be in this email? Easy: what you achieved (obviously, especially if you've finished a task that they gave you); your rough plan for the upcoming week; issues and questions which your boss needs to provide some input on; anything interesting which has come up that they should be aware of. Done. It normally takes less than thirty minutes, can be done just before going home, lets you boast about stuff you've done really well, and will impress your manager immensely.

Words and letters: Communicating effectively

Pretty much every 'knowledge' based job, (i.e. everything in the pharmaceutical world), relies on communication. Everyone has their own jobs and specialisation, which means that actually achieving anything requires a lot of back and forth communication – if you can't communicate, you can't do your job. In practice this means writing documents, writing emails, using the phone well, and, yes, a lot of meetings (for more on meetings, see pg. 55).

Writing documents

You will end up writing many, many documents once you enter the pharmaceutical industry. Standard GMP rules require that almost everything gets documented ("if it wasn't documented, it wasn't done", cries the FDA as they audit your site). To that you can add study protocols, validation reports, regulatory dossiers, update emails, and more – all the writing you could ever hope to have in your life. So you'll have to get used to business writing. This is very different to the academic writing style you've been reading (and writing) in publications, it's all about getting the facts across as simply as possible. You want to be accurate, clear, and concise. No-one has enough time (you included) to wade through a page of flowery text to get to the actual point of the message, no-one wants the sort of misunderstandings that happen when the document is badly written.

Good writing comes as much from planning as from actual skill, and both of these can be learned. With any document the first thing to identify is the target audience – for regulatory this would be agencies such as the FDA, for QC the document is normally for internal use, marketing will write for outside groups. Often you'll have several target groups, and you need to know what that audience would like to know from the document.

The next step is to gather the source data. Using regulatory affairs as an example, you'll need study reports from development and manufacturing, validation data from quality control, maybe even batch release certificates. Go out and collect this information, making sure you put everything you've gathered into a folder that is both well-organised and easily accessible by everyone later. Speaking from personal experience, there is nothing worse than trawling through badly-organised folders put together over a decade ago while trying to find long-lost source data. Be organised, your future co-workers will thank you!

Information gathered and audience identified? Write an outline showing what goes where – you'll often be able to use previous documents from the company for this as well. Then start filling in the document with actual data, actual text, connecting paragraphs and explanatory sentences – basically everything that makes a document more than just a list of tables. This is a first draft, so once you're done you should go back over it with an eye for problems and mismatched details. What sort of details? This depends on your role but it will often be things involving correctly labelled specifications, whether information matches between different documents, whether the information present matches documents which were previously used for official submissions. Sound complex? It is.

Document style
Most pharmaceutical companies will have a set 'style' that needs to be used in anything official – often to the point of having custom templates or add-ins for Word or PowerPoint. Although it may be ugly or highly irritating to use, you are stuck with it and so will have to learn. Spend a bit of time looking at other reports to see how it should be put together, play around with the template to see what header looks like what. Figure it out and stick to it.

If, however, you're one of those lucky ones in a small company without any official standards, then try to rein in your creativity. It's still a *business* document, so it should be in 'boring' colours, try to avoid bright purple headings if you can. Having said that, experiment a bit to try and make something that is both interesting to look at and professional, it may not seem like much but people will be far happier to read 'slightly-interesting-looking' reports than boring ones.

Document review and signing

You may have written the document, but this is still just the first draft – now it's time for document review! Normally your manager will do the first review of the document, technical branches will often have reviews from people in QA, regulatory, and production as well. They will most likely have a lot to say. It can be depressing when your beautifully crafted document comes back, red lines and track changes all over the place, comments added saying things like 'what is this?' or 'we need to talk'. You'll probably be angry or thinking about making some sort of nasty comment to the reviewers. Don't. It's both stupid and unprofessional. Instead take a deep breath and remember that they just want the document to be the best it can be. Go get a coffee. When you get back, look over the comments again – which ones make sense, which don't you agree with? Accept the first, think about the second. Call up your reviewers and use the screen-sharing ability of your instant messaging program (e.g. many large companies use Skype for Business) to run through your changes and get their opinions. If you really disagree about an approach, then organise a follow-up meeting – reviewers will often have different opinions about the information the document should present and so will need to work out a compromise between themselves.

Once everyone is happy (or at least equally annoyed) then the document will often be signed (this is a requirement for GxP documents and so you will likely spend a lot of time doing this). Most companies use electronic signatures on PDFs for documents, some still print copies out and pass them back and forth. Once the document is signed, however, it becomes an official, fixed item – no changes allowed. This means that the specification error you discover two months later will require a full amendment and second signing round to fix – try to catch all these mistakes before they happen!

Writing emails

The number of emails you'll send and receive depends a lot on your job. Communication-heavy roles such as regulatory affairs will find their inboxes maxing out quickly, others will have a lower load. Make no mistake though, pharmaceutical jobs thrive on communication and that usually comes down to emailing. We cover the best approaches to dealing with *incoming* email elsewhere in the book (pg. 65), but a few general points apply from a communication perspective: Email is usually less time-critical than a phone call, you can get away with only checking it two or three times per day. *But* you should always try to reply to an email you get within 24 hours – even if it's something to say 'I've added it to my list but can't give you an answer this week'. Not being able to do a task is also important information for people to know, if only so they can ask someone else to do it.

So how do you write a good 'business' email? Keep it short and easy to read, use bullet-points if there a lot of things you need to get across. Use **bold font** on important bits of information, because it stands out of the crowd. Never send several emails if one will do, no-one enjoys inbox spam. Always make sure you read the email *before* you send it – check for spelling mistakes, that it has enough information, and that you haven't accidentally just sent your complaint about the empty coffee pot to the entire company.

If you end up on a group email, with several people on CC, you need to decide if it's an important email or an announcement email. If you want to reply to someone announcing something (new job, etc.) then there's no need to keep everyone in the loop, hit 'reply'. If it's a group round where some sort of decision is being made or information is being gathered, use reply-all. Although it may seem a bit counterproductive to have large mailing groups, many people in the pharma world will get angry if they are cut out of decision-making loops. This can even be considered an office-politics type of move – try to avoid this! Keep everyone who was involved, involved.

The other thing you do have to watch out for is the Angry Email. You know what I mean, someone writes something insulting your work, asking why you haven't gotten anything done for the last few days (even though you've been slaving away at several things), telling you that the last document was a waste of time and you should redo it. Sound familiar? The temptation is to write back and tell them where to go, or at the very least to make it very clear why they are wrong. Don't do it. Seriously, writing that angry email will make you feel better for about half an hour and then will lead to many weeks in an unhappy workplace – well after everyone has forgotten what the original point of it all was. Always have a pause before you reply to *those* emails. Wait an hour or a day, write your scathing reply and then delete it, it doesn't matter – just make sure there's some sort of pause before you actually send it out.

Phone calls

A phone call or teleconference is a way to pass on information or solve problems – it requires more effort than email but the information flow rate is much higher when people are speaking to each other. You will end up spending a lot of time on the phone, particularly if you're in a communication-heavy role such as regulatory or sales. It's thus important to use your phone calls well – don't let them become another time waster like emails can be.

An important phone call or teleconference should be thought of as a *meeting* (which, in fact, it is). Be prepared beforehand, have your notes and information together, have a clear idea of what you want to accomplish with the call. Take notes – who you spoke to, what you spoke about, what decisions or tasks came out of it (particularly if you are meant to be doing something!). Avoid the temptation to do other work while half-listening to a teleconference, you are guaranteed to miss something important and other people *will* notice. Give it just as much attention as you would if everyone were face to face.

If something is *urgent*, then it should be communicated via phone. Emails can be forgotten, instant messaging can be ignored, but a ringing phone will get attention like nothing else. Naturally this will also pull people out of concentration on their current task, so if possible you should organise to call at a set time. If it's truly urgent though, call. Just don't waste their time. What does this mean? Be direct with what you need, don't go on about pointless things for ages while their attention slowly drifts back to the previous task. Aim to have a single, clear goal, timeline and reason for your phone call that you can tell the person you have called – e.g. 'I need these batch records by this afternoon otherwise the submission will fail'. This gets the urgency of your problem across and avoids clouding the issue with other commentary.

Lastly, don't be scared of the telephone. It can be incredibly nerve-wracking calling people up, (especially when you know they don't want to talk to you) – but as with everything in life, it won't get easier if you leave it for later. Do it, get it over with, and with time you'll wonder why you were ever nervous.

More than talking: Meetings and conferences

The biggest plus point about academia and your PhD is that there are basically no meetings. Seriously, it's basically nothing. Just wait until you get into industry. Because meetings make up such a large portion of the pharma world, you need to know how to cope with them and how to use them effectively. We'll look at it from two points of view, the meetings you are attending and the meeting you are hosting.

Attending a meeting

The most important rule is easy: turn up early. Not just-in-time, actually early. This prevents unforeseen difficulties making you late and lets you chat to the other people present prior to the meeting, something which is often more useful than the meeting itself. Take a moment to introduce yourself to people you don't know or catch up with others, this will make you more comfortable in their presence and thus more willing to contribute.

As with almost everything at work, it's better to be prepared – meetings are no different. You should know before the meeting what it will be about – what the aim of the meeting is and what it hopes to achieve. If you don't know, ask – but do it politely ("is there a point to this?" is the Wrong Way). Try to figure out if you will be required to bring information or a certain viewpoint to the meeting, then make sure you have that information. If you are speaking, keep on track and don't wander off topic. Modify the tone and pace of your words to keep people interested. Know a boring monotone speaker? Or someone who rambles on about nothing particularly useful? Don't do that.

Having said that, new employees will generally be attending meetings with the assumption that they will learn things, take notes, and generally stay out of the way. This means that you'll be listening more than you're talking, especially in larger meetings where upper management is attending. Take notes of what's happening, be it pen and paper or electronic notes (though the clicking of keys on a laptop may irritate people). Not only does note-taking stop you falling asleep (a very important plus) but you'll be able to write down all of the acronyms and terms which you've never heard before so you can ask people later.

After the meeting, look at what you wrote down. Try to get it into a more manageable format, preferably into some sort of online notebook – if nothing else make sure you'll be able to read it a few months down the track. Stick any useful information into your long term notes, add any tasks you have to do onto your list. It's usually best to do this within a day or two so you don't forget everything.

Hosting a meeting

There are a lot of meetings in pharma, and it's almost a certainty that at some stage you will have to lead a meeting yourself. Remember all those times you complained about how boring that meeting was, or how it went on and on with no real conclusion? Karma, baby! Now you have to avoid the same mistakes.

Decide the topic and agenda

The first and most important question you should ask yourself is 'why are we having this meeting?' Is it to discuss an issue, solve a problem, keep people informed of progress, etc.? Is it actually necessary to hold a meeting, could you just email everyone with a status update or document to review? Remember that every meeting being held costs money (the sum of all attendees' hourly wages) and time (which is even more precious). Be sure you really need a meeting before you host one.

If a meeting is necessary, however, then it needs to be organised. Put together a list of the topics you want to discuss. Make sure it's a detailed list, it shouldn't be something like 'discuss recent batch release', it should state what exactly you want to discuss and what decisions you want to make. Order the list from most important topic through to least important. This is now your agenda, it should be sent around to everyone who will attend the meeting. Try to send it at least the day before the meeting, it allows everyone to look into the subject themselves and do some thinking before the big event.

Decide who should attend

Only invite people who are *directly* involved with the project or issue which will be discussed. Note that I said directly, not 'could be interested' or 'may be involved in three months'. An invitation to a meeting carries a certain expectation that the person being invited will attend, which means that they will then have to justify why the meeting would be a waste of their time. Be nice, don't force uninvolved people to attend the meeting – send them the minutes afterwards to keep them up to date and they'll thank you for not wasting their time.

Running the meeting

Most important – be punctual. Start on time, end on time. This can be difficult in some cases as many people will run late and not reach the meeting room in time. Ignore this, and start without them. Why? Because you are indirectly punishing people who arrive on time by making them wait around for someone who is late – and this almost guarantees that they won't feel any pressure to be punctual next time around. Start on time, let the latecomers catch up when they arrive.

Once the meeting has begun, you need to be enthusiastic about leading it. Attendees take their cues from the person up the front – if you don't care, they won't either. Similarly you need to make sure everyone is involved in the discussion; people who feel left out will tune out and stop paying attention to the entire thing. Your job is difficult, you need to keep everyone involved, but not let anyone get *too* involved – no arguments, no long-winded blabbering from people who don't recognise the point. Feel free to step in and pull everyone back on track whenever you need to, nothing kills productivity like a meeting going off the rails.

At the end of the meeting, usually in the last five minutes or so, you should restate what decisions you've made and what tasks have been assigned. This is a good way to ensure that everyone knows what to do (even those that stopped paying attention) and will avoid those arguments weeks later when someone claims that they were never told what they should do.

Send the minutes around afterwards

Nothing wastes time quite as well as repeatedly going over the same decisions in every meeting, week after week. You can avoid this by sending everyone that attended a summary of the meeting, including decisions made and tasks assigned – this is usually known as the **meeting minutes**.

Because you will rapidly forget the details of any meeting, you should try to get your notes into a reasonable summary within an hour or two of finishing. This summary should include the people who attended, what was discussed, which major/minor decisions were made, and what actions/tasks were decided on as part of that. Send it around to the attendees, keep a copy for yourself, and put your tasks on your task list. Just doing this step puts you ahead of 80% of the crowd, and yes, this will be noticed by your managers.

Lunch

Not really a meeting, I know. But it's still pretty important to go out to lunch with the rest of your colleagues, don't just sit at the desk slaving away. Why? Well for a start, work isn't everything, and you need to have a life. Second, so much in your career will come from who you know and what people think of you – depressing, yes, but that's how it is. People would generally prefer to give the promotion to the person they see at lunch every couple of days over the one who eats alone at their desk. Why? Because they're (a) a friendlier presence and (b) obviously competent and efficient enough that they don't *need* to work during lunch.

Conferences

Conferences are one of those things you'll see a lot of as an academic and not much of if you're working for a pharma company. Unless you're in marketing or sales, in which case you'll be sick of them after about a month or two. But conferences are nonetheless an excellent opportunity for people who want to grow their career, they provide information *and contacts* which you simply can't get in any other way.

Realistically, your employers are unlikely to pay for a conference – especially when you're new to the company. That's ok, some things you'll have to consider an investment in your career and just pay yourself (it's usually a tax deduction though, so don't miss the opportunity there!). Pick a conference that's nearby, has a theme which you consider suitable for your long-term career, and just go.

Just remember that a conference is a waste of time if you're not there to talk to people, so you'll have to be a bit outgoing and go introduce yourself. Bring some business cards along – if you can't get work-related ones then get your own, even just with your name and email. Business cards are super cheap to buy online (think of it as three days' worth of coffee) and they tell the people you meet that you are a Proper Professional. Hand them out like candy, talk to people, ask for their contact details, look them up on LinkedIn, ask people what they do, how they got there, where they're going. Tell them what you do and where you're going. You'd be amazed how many useful people you meet and how many random career paths you'll open up by simply impressing people at conferences. So go on, give it a try.

Written memory: Taking notes

Every pharma job has a focus on *knowledge management* –
knowing stuff and then figuring out what to do based on that
knowledge. But the things you need to know will come at you very
quickly, often in a giant pile of other pointless information during
the course of a long and winding meeting. This means that you
have to be able to record information and tasks as they come in
rather than hoping that you'll remember later on. Hence – note
taking.

The decisions between handwritten and electronic notes is one of
personal preference – try both and see which one you prefer.
Electronic notes (think OneNote, Evernote, etc.) have the
advantage of being easy to search through and simple to back up.
Handwritten notes are quieter to make (avoiding the clicky-keys-
in-the-meeting problem), allow more free-form note-taking and
have been suggested to improve recall after the fact. Some people
use both, converting handwritten into electronic format as they go
over the notes after the meeting. We'll cover a few tips for all of
these below.

Electronic notes

Electronic notebook programs such as OneNote or Evernote are
great for organising large amounts of information in an easily
searchable way. These programs usually offer shared notebooks
(so everyone can collaborate) and often link into email and
browser software to let you save information from almost
everywhere. This makes them extremely useful when dealing with
the multitude of email-based information which you'll receive
during your day – simply send important information directly to
the notebook. Their utility for taking notes during meetings
depends a lot on the hardware you have – tablets are very useful,
laptops are great if you are a fast typist, desktops are obviously
not so practical.

Electronic notebooks are set up as a number of hierarchical
'books' and 'pages', allowing you to group your topics as needed.

This approach tends to force more order onto your notes than the equivalent paper version, few people will have a completely separate paper notebook for each topic in their work. They also have the major advantage of being able to add hyperlinks between individual notebook pages to move quickly from one page to another. Use this wherever you can to help in navigating your notes – link a page of meeting notes to the larger page for the topic, cross-link two related document reviews to each other, etc.

This ordered approach also extends to the notes themselves – you will tend to write more lists or lines than the freeform notes or back-and-forth arrows possible with handwriting. Take advantage of this forced order by setting up template notes for your most typical tasks. As an example, those who do a lot of change evaluations will find that they regularly need to record similar information (reference numbers, due dates, affected documents). By setting up a template which contains set locations for all of this 'standard' data you will be able to simply make a new page and go directly into filling in the gaps. This has multiple benefits: you can work more efficiently, it is much simpler to understand your previous work (as opposed to the freeform chaos you will otherwise end up with), and you are far more likely to spot gaps in the work. Similar templates can be set up for meetings, weekly task lists, your weekly update for your manager, etc.

Those who want more flexibility may want to look into mind-mapping software. Mind-maps are essentially a hierarchical diagram, containing a central topic with branches to various subtopics, then further subtopics, etc. (you will undoubtedly see this in action in a professional development seminar, probably with big sheets of paper and coloured pens). Actually getting the hang of making a mind-map will take a bit of practice – particularly in getting the hang of making the most relevant problem the centre of the map. It also tends to be slightly slower than simply typing, however it then has later advantages when it comes to seeing relationships between key topics and fostering creative ideas.

The most common way of entering notes into the system is with the trusty keyboard – which means that you need to know how to type well. Can you touch-type? Now is the time to learn! Beyond this shorthand is a valuable timesaver (just like in handwritten notes). Make up your own acronyms or letter combinations (drawn squiggles obviously don't work so well here), use txt-abbreviations if you want. At the same time, be careful that you pay enough attention to the meeting itself. The laptop in front of you can act as a psychological barrier to discussion, as well as being a distracting source of new emails, instant messages, etc. Tablets are a good work-around here, being unobtrusive yet allowing direct electronic note-taking – the requirement not to check your emails, however, remains with you.

Handwritten notes: legible, not pretty

The other side of the coin is to take handwritten notes, writing into a notebook or equivalent. This works well for meetings and other situations where you are 'offline' but isn't particularly helpful when you are dealing with emailed information.

Unless you are amazing with shorthand you will not be able to write down exactly what people are saying. Instead you have to concentrate and pick out the important themes, in particular facts and tasks, and then record them in your own words. Keep things simple and short, don't attempt to write long sentences and beautiful paragraphs of prose. You should also remember that a notebook is non-linear, you can write pretty much wherever you want. This means that you can include very large margins on each page (think 20-25% of the total page) to let yourself come back and write important follow-ups, summaries, big arrows pointing out what you need, etc. etc. You can add boxes at the bottom to contain summaries of your page, draw in mind-maps to cover certain topics, use images to draw attention to important points. Simply try out a few methods and see what works best for you.

One thing to be watch out for, however, and that is the temptation to take exquisitely written notes, highlighted in multiple colours, with lines framing important points. Don't. Not only will you miss half of what's going on while choosing the correct colour pen, the 'highlighting' approach has been shown to be relatively inefficient at helping your recall after the meeting. Feel free to write badly, with grammatically terrible sentences and squiggly arrows crossing the entire page – the important thing is that you can decipher those notes later on.

As you get to know the job you just started, you'll notice that several phrases come up often enough that it's not worth writing them down each time. Feel free to use acronyms as you take notes (e.g. why write 'follow-up stability testing' when you could write FUST?), make up little symbols that mean 'you need to do this' or 'this is important information', learn shorthand if you're really dedicated. Just remember what your little abbreviations stand for so you don't need to spend half an hour staring at something like '2-a BRI' before you remember what it stands for.

Lastly, there is one major disadvantage of handwritten notes as compared to electronic, and this is the inability to easily search through and find previous information. You can mitigate this by making your own index page, either by numbering pages and making a list in the back or by making a visual index listing. How does this work? Turn to the back page of the notebook, this will be your 'searchable' index. When you have a meeting or need to take notes it will normally relate to a keyword or two – think of 'process validation' or 'major customer X'. Write this keyword on the back page in a single vertical list. Now mark the edge of the page that your notes are on in such a way that the mark is at the same height as the keyword in the index list and (importantly) the mark can be seen when the notebook is closed. When you come back later, open to the index page and look for your keyword – every set of notes relating to that keyword will have a mark on the edge of the page at the same height as the keyword is written. And there you go – searchable notes.

Converting handwritten to electronic notes

Taking notes is useless if you don't actually do anything with that information, and this is where you need to convert your scribble into something more useful. A time consuming but effective approach is to take written notes and then convert them to an electronic format for ease of searching and organising. This can be thought of as an intermediate processing step as you take your raw notes and convert them to action items and information to remember.

How do you do this? First go through and check for things you need to do (here's where those symbols come in handy) – these should go onto your task list with some commentary as to why you're doing it. Next, look for important information, this should be filed away somewhere within your electronic notebook. You can have pages for different studies, document reviews, customer notes, it doesn't matter as long as you can *find the information again* (although given how good search functions are getting it's almost impossible to lose information once it's in there). Lastly go over the notes you took a third time, looking at everything that's left. Is it important, related to a task, possibly something that will come back in a month to bite you in the arse? Then you should move it into the electronic format. If in doubt, keep it.

A faster approach, albeit without the 'processing' side, is simply to use your smartphone to take a picture of the notes and then forward it to your system. OneNote and Evernote are both capable of searching handwritten text, though the accuracy obviously depends on the quality of your handwriting. Once the picture is present in your system, go ahead and pull out your tasks and move them to your to-do list.

Beating stress: Staying on top of your workload

You will have a lot more work to do in your industry career than you did in your academic one. Simple as that. There are many different projects running simultaneously, tight timelines, too few employees, too much usage of horrible words like 'preponing' (where management decides that you could do things earlier than planned – so work harder you lazy swine!). This in turn means that you need to keep on top of all of this work – surviving the flood of emails, to-do items and assorted task requests which will inevitably surface at the worst possible time. How? Well, you can read this section, as it will provide some advice on how to avoid being overwhelmed.

Dealing with email

You will receive many, many, many emails once you've started in industry – enough that you will often wish that people would just go away and stop contacting you for a while so that you can do your actual work. Sadly this will never happen – you will always get more emails (except on Christmas Day, maybe). Instead, you need to learn how to cope with and use the oncoming flood of emails to succeed in your job.

Many people fall into the trap of using their inbox as a general to-do list. The usual result is that their inboxes end up stuffed with a thousand emails, nothing can be found because it's all 'in there somewhere' and it takes forever to get things done. Don't be this person! In particular watch out for the moment where you think 'I'll get back to that later'. You won't. Or if you do, you'll waste just as much time reading the email again and figuring out what you should do.

Instead, use the following approach:

Check your email a couple of times a day

You don't need to have your email client sitting in the corner of the window, constantly beeping whenever something comes in.

And you certainly don't need to check your inbox the moment something happens. This will simply distract you from whatever you were doing and forces you to get your mind back on track after reading the email. So check it two or three times a day. In between, just ignore the inbox. Worried about missing something important? If it's really important, someone will call you and ask for help (believe me, they'll call). This applies to you as well – if you want something urgently, call someone.

Do your emails in batches and triage as you go

Do your emails in one big batch, several times a day – this lets you get everything done without constant minor distractions. As you work through the emails, take a moment to think about each one you are reading. Is it information you should keep? Is it a task or action you need to do? Is it a bit of information or a document which you want to read or go over at a later stage? Is it relevant to you? Is it unimportant? Based on this, you then decide on the appropriate action:

Is the email unimportant, not relevant, trying to sell something, or otherwise useless?
Delete it. Smile when you do it, if you like. Just make sure you delete it, because there is no point to having it clogging up your inbox.

Is it something you would like to read at a later stage, but not now?
This includes reports from other parts of the company, random FYI's, and the like. Ask yourself (and be honest) – are you *really* going to get around to reading this, given the other things you have in your 'when I have spare time' list? No? Delete it. Yes? Move the email into another folder set aside for these spare-time items, and come back to it when you can. Make sure you clean this folder out every six months or so, lest you end up finding long-forgotten and woefully out-of-date reports next time you open it up.

Is it information which is relevant to you?
If yes, immediately add it to your information-keeping system, such as an OneNote electronic notebook or similar. This can be a short sentence, a paragraph, linked files or even the entire email pasted in wholesale – the important thing is that you can quickly find it again later. Again, file it right away. Leaving it until later means that information will get lost somewhere in between you reading the email and your boss asking you about it. Once you've filed the information, store the email (if it is something important) or delete it.

Is it a task or action for you?
If yes, how long will it take to do? A good rule of thumb is that everything that would take less than two minutes to do should be done right away. It would take longer for you to come back to it, read the email, figure out what to do, and do it than it would to simply do it right now. Longer tasks should be put onto your to-do list – determine how important this new action is, then slot it in amongst all the others. If it is not the most important thing you could be doing *right now*, then put it on your list and do it later.

Do it once, but do it all

By filing, deleting, and responding to emails, you should aim to get your inbox as close to empty as humanly possible. Don't use it as a storage location for action items or things which you will look at later. Instead think of your inbox as a temporary collection point for items which will then be processed and dealt with. The acronym 'OHIO', for Only Handle It Once, is an excellent one to keep in mind when trawling through your giant list of incoming emails. It represents the idea that each incoming email or piece of paperwork should be picked up once, dealt with, and then put away. Don't waste time repeating your actions and don't clutter up your inbox with unread rubbish – read it, classify it, and deal with it. Then go back to your real work.

Time management

This is an enormous subject which has been the focus of more books, websites, and talks than can be listed. So we're just going to give you the most important things here. One very important thing first: you'll never have everything done, you'll never have a completely empty task list. And the moment you do, someone will come and dump another project on you. Industry can create work for you faster than you can do it. Plan to do your best despite this.

Plan ahead, plan specifics

The most important part of managing your time is planning, and the most important part of planning is looking at specifics. Get into the habit of taking ten to fifteen minutes every evening to plan out what you will need to achieve the next day. Be specific. Don't write 'finish report', write 'finish section 5, get signatures' – specific tasks are much easier to work towards than general ones. This applies to larger projects as well – if you know you have a project coming up, break it down into specific mini-tasks. Prioritise, and then do them. Large projects don't need to be completed in one giant burst of effort – these mini-tasks can be completed a piece at a time over the next few weeks amongst your other work.

You should always try to work on your *most important task first*. Never work on low-priority things when you have a high-priority task waiting for you, unless you are utterly certain that you will manage the main task afterwards. Not sure which of your tasks is the most important one? Ask your co-workers and your boss – it is often easier to say what other people should be working on than what you should work on yourself.

Because of this, the most useful information you can have when planning is to know the priority and timeline for each task, project, or request. Get into the habit of simply asking 'when do you need this done?' whenever you get a request or a task. If their due date is reasonable, no worries. If it's not enough time, then ask what sort of priority this task has – then you need to decide if your schedule should be rearranged or if you should push back and ask for more time. An important corollary here is that if something can go wrong, it will. Probably around the same time as six deadlines come due and the FDA drops by for an inspection. Always be on the lookout for things which *may* go wrong – identify them, plan ahead, and figure out alternative options for the moment that they do go wrong.

The other part of planning ahead involves focusing on opportunities rather than problems. Looking at how the project is going, what's the likely outcome? Will there be follow-up work? Further studies? Take a moment to briefly think about where you could take your project from here, and write down a couple of ideas or plans. Although this may seem fairly pointless in an entry position, one of the big things which will help you move upwards in the company is the ability to see beyond your immediate tasks.

Don't procrastinate

Planning is great, planning without actually doing what you plan to do is stupid. How do you solve this tendency towards procrastination? Simple rule: Do It Now. Not tomorrow, not next week, just do it now. If there's a problem, address it now. Document to write? Do it. Presentation to put together? Yep, do it. Tasks which get put off too long become problems, problems put off too long become crises. Just do whatever you need to do and get it over with. It won't get better with time.

Start with the hard stuff

There are two ways of looking at the tasks you have to do. One is to start with the hardest and most important task first, the moment you get going in the morning – this will ensure that you are working on the problem while you are (a) most awake/fresh and (b) more likely to finish the important stuff if something else comes up during the day. The second approach involves starting with smaller tasks and then, as you complete them, using that momentum to work your way up to larger things.

Generally the first approach is better, that of beginning with the first task. This is because your day is rarely well-organised and if something is likely to go wrong it will at around 10-11am, just when the momentum approach is starting to pay off. However, if you're fairly certain that you won't be interrupted and you have difficulties diving straight in, then give the second approach a try and see if it works for you.

Get away from unnecessary meetings

Sometimes you'll have days which are simply non-stop meetings from start to end (this becomes more of a problem as you move up in the firm, but it will still happen in your first few months). Some meetings are simply not worth your time, and will do nothing but fill up the day. If you can (i.e. if your manager hasn't expressly told you to go) try to avoid meetings where you aren't really required. This doesn't mean that you should just not turn up! Instead you should get into the habit of asking *why* a meeting is being conducted and what your *specific role* would be. If there's no good answer to these questions, try asking if there isn't a better way for the information to be communicated to you – phone, email, casual coffee. Sometimes this isn't possible, of course (welcome to industry!). But if you find that one or two meetings are consistently blocking your productivity, it might be worth talking to your manager to see whether attendance is truly necessary or whether your priorities should be elsewhere.

Book time for yourself

You'll always have a lot of things to do, and it is often very difficult to focus on the important things while everyone is sending you emails, calling, asking for document reviews – all the small things which very quickly add up into a day flying past before you realise. Because of that you need to find a way to do the work you *need* to do, rather than the work you are being *asked* to do.

The best way to achieve this is to block out a section of time on your own calendar – think of it as making a meeting for one person. Make sure your status is set to Busy, don't look at your email and don't pick up the phone. Use this time to focus work on the things which really need to be done, and don't let anything distract you from the task. If you are able to block out even just an hour every second day or even every day, you'll find that you can work through a lot of otherwise impossible-to-complete tasks on your to-do list. Book time for yourself, not just meetings with others.

Use the downtime

There's busy times at work, but there are also quiet times, often in the middle of summer or around the holidays. It's tempting to slack off and use some of the accumulated overtime, and to be honest you definitely should take this chance. But at the same time, take the opportunity to catch up on all those little things which simply aren't urgent enough to do during the busy periods. Get your paperwork organised, think about long-term hypothetical goals, put together a plan for the next year, think about your career. Now that you have a bit of breathing room, use it to think long-term.

Looking back: the weekly recap

Just as important as planning ahead is looking back at what you've done. Normally the week flies by in a number of minor crises and major projects, and it's often difficult to look back a month or two and figure out just what you actually did.

So how do you keep track of the past as it happens? The easiest way is a weekly recap. On Friday afternoon, when everything starts winding down and half the people leave early, take an hour or so and look at the week that's just gone by. What did you spend most of your time doing? What have you achieved? Did you spend your time on important things, or unimportant tasks? What have you learned this week, and where can you improve on things? Write it all down, make a simple bullet-point list. It doesn't have to be fancy, but you want to *think* about what you've done rather than reacting to emergencies as they come. Make sure you store the recap somewhere that you can find it easily again.

Why should you bother with this when you'd rather just go home? Well, from a purely selfish point of view, your yearly bonus will be based on how many examples you can use to support your own cleverness and efficiency – this is obviously much easier to do when you've got a record of some sort. More importantly: you'll be learning and doing a lot in the first few years. Being able to record these lessons as you're doing them will help immensely as you try to take everything in – and writing this information in an easily retrievable place lets you hunt down important information without too much stress.

What's the other major bonus of putting this together? You can use it as the basis of your weekly update to your boss, where you which you can read about in more detail on pg. 45.

Organise everything: Planning successful projects

Most of the work you'll end up doing will be project-based, by which we mean that it will involve a number of tasks which need to be completed in order to achieve a final, large goal. This could be something like writing up a large stability report, completing the QA release for a drug batch, or putting together a regulatory document. To get the final product out, you need to be able to plan out a number of interlinked tasks in a way that takes a minimum amount of time. How do we go about this?

What tasks do you need to do?

First identify all of the work which you need to do to complete the project. You have to be really, really clear on what is actually required at the end of the project or you will find yourself turning out a beautiful piece of work that no-one actually wants. It's often a good idea to have a short meeting with the people who are assigning you the project (think of them as your clients) to discuss the goals, problems to be solved, and the budget (in resources such as time, people, and money).

Put it all in order

Without worrying about how long everything will take, put all of the tasks identified above in order. What task needs to happen first, which one needs to be done before the next, what can run in parallel and what needs to be consecutive? There are a number of methods out there for determining this kind of information (Gantt and Pert charts being two of the common ones) but you can also get away with scribbling a flow chart on some paper for small projects. Just don't lose the paper!

Get the team involved

If you're working with other people, now's the time to get them together for a meeting to go over your work so far – do they think it makes sense? What are their estimates for time to complete each tasks? Does everyone agree on which tasks are sequential and which are parallel? Having several sets of eyes on the project plan will minimise the number of errors which sneak through.

Estimate times for each task

This step can be incredibly hand-wavy or highly detailed, depending on how much information you have available. Look at each task individually, and list all of the information you have regarding that task (this includes hard data and guesstimates from team members, just keep a record of where the information came from). Now start estimating, using a combination of several methods:

Bottom-up estimation involves breaking each task down into smaller and smaller tasks, figuring out how long the smallest of these tasks would take to complete, and then adding those numbers together. It can be very accurate, but will take a lot longer than less detailed methods.

Top-down estimation takes previous experience (from similar projects or the like) and uses that to make a guesstimate as to how long each project stage will take. This is frequently amazingly inaccurate, but gives you a fast estimate which you can compare against numbers from other methods as a reality check.

Parametric estimation involves estimating how long one task will take, then multiplying by how many tasks there are. Obviously this only works if the tasks themselves are very similar, but makes a quick and easy planning method.

Three-point estimation is also known as best/worse/base case estimation – you should end up with three different times required based on everything going well (hah), everything going terribly, and the most likely outcome. The final 'time expected' is usually calculated as the sum of the optimistic time, pessimistic time, and 4-times the likely time, all divided by six. More concisely:

$$T_{(expected)} = (T_{(optimistic)} + 4 * T_{(likely)} + T_{(pessimistic)}) / 6.$$

Yes, this is mathematics, welcome to project management! Three-point estimation is more complex than the other methods and requires a bit more work, but it allows you to make much more realistic plans than otherwise possible.

There are a few things to watch out for when estimating times. First, anyone working full-time on a project is actually only working on it for about 80% of the day. There's emails, meetings, emergencies, sick cats – many things will nibble away at the amount of time people can use to work on a project. So stick with 80%. Also be careful when planning out times for people who are working on several projects at once – there is always a 'switching cost' when changing from one project to another and this will also pull productivity down from the ideal number which you are planning with.

Finished estimating times? Good, now go and find your manager, co-worker, team members, and ask them to tear the timeline apart. If you can successfully defend your proposed timelines against a group of people asking a bunch of nasty questions then you've probably got a realistic set of assumptions.

Make the project schedule
Figured out how long each task will take, as well as the order they need to be performed? Top show! Now put all of this together into a project schedule for everyone to refer to – this is what you will use to keep the project on track and to determine what everyone involved should be doing. Unless you are dealing with a very complex project, the easiest way to show this is with a Gantt chart.

What's a Gantt chart? Here's an example of one which would be used for an application to extend the shelf life of a drug which your company is producing. First the stability sample needs to be taken out of the storage room it has been sitting in all this time – this is the first step in the project. Analytical testing is performed in the next two weeks, but as results come in over time we can already start preparing the stability report while this is going on. The final, signed report can only be completed once all data is in, so this happens in week 4. Regulatory affairs can start preparing their documents with the raw data from analytics, but can only finalise their dossier updates once the corresponding report is finished – hence the week 6 task. Once finalised, the regulatory variation can then be submitted to the FDA, closing out the project.

An example Gantt chart showing the subprojects and timing required for a shelf-life extension variation

Task	Week 1	Week 2	Week 3	Week 4	Week 5	Week 6	Week 7
Remove stability sample from storage	■						
Perform analytical tests		■	■				
Prepare stability report			■				
Finalise report				■			
Prepare regulatory variation				■	■		
Finalise regulatory variation						■	
Submit variation to FDA							■

Be realistic with deadlines

Always, always, always *overestimate* the amount of time it will take you to do something. This is important when doing your own planning but is *vital* when telling your manager how long something will take. Tight deadlines are at the mercy of something going wrong (and something always goes wrong) and no-one, particularly management, will be impressed when you bring in a project right on time for a tight deadline. However if you miss a deadline, then people start to get angry and question your competence. We can easily see the consequences in the following, highly scientific table.

This highly technical table demonstrates why you should always overestimate timelines

	Pessimistic timeline	Optimistic timeline
Project done in short amount of time	Better than expected – management is impressed	Project completed as expected – no-one cares
Project takes longer than expected	Project completed as expected – no-one cares	You done goofed – management is angry

The moral of the story here is that when asked for a timeline on project completion, you should *always* err on the side of pessimism. First look at the project you're being asked to do – be realistic about how much of your time this will take. Then look at your current workload – can you fit in this extra time? Do other things need to be shuffled out of the way? Use this to estimate how long it will take to complete the task. Then add a safety factor to account for Things Going Wrong – a good rule of thumb is 20% on top if you know exactly what you're doing, 100% on top if you've never done it before. Then provide this final number to whoever asked you for the timeline alongside a list of the tasks which you need to push aside to achieve this. Why? Because you will often have competing priorities, and you need to make it clear just what other tasks will be affected by this new project.

Now do it

Finished planning? Good work! Now you should actually do everything. Pass tasks to everyone, take up your own tasks (no, you can't slack off while everyone else does the work) and get to work.

Make sure that you track your progress as you go – are you meeting your deadlines and project milestones? What about the others? This is the sort of thing you should check daily, because it will give you an early warning of any potential delays or lost time. Use this information to help prioritise your to-do list, which tasks need to be done now, which can be delayed? Plan out the time you have for the week, then for the day, keeping in mind that some time will be wasted by things such as meetings and spontaneous problems.

Prioritised? Good, now do the work! Always work on the item or task which has the highest priority, this is normally something which is both important and urgent. Don't get distracted by easy, low-priority tasks or unimportant work, go straight for the high-priority work. There's rarely enough time in the day to do everything, so you're better off getting the important stuff done first.

Don't forget to communicate with your teammates and your manager as you go along – keep everyone updated on task completion, how the project is going, when there's a risk or delay or when there's the chance you'll be done early. Everything in industry comes down to teamwork and the basis of teamwork is communication. So keep talking!

Wrap up the project

One art that many people forget is the act of wrapping up the project once it is finished. This is not meant in the sense of sending off the document to management or submitting the dossier to the FDA, (though you should definitely take the moment to party a bit). Instead it involves thinking about what you did, where it went well, and where it could be better.

Another common term for this is debriefing, it simply involves gathering all of the team together for a short post-project meeting to discuss how everything went. If you were managing the project, then you should consider this your last duty – bring a cake along to celebrate and aim to get the honest opinions out of everyone that was involved. How well did the project go? Were the goals and deadlines met? What went really well? What went badly? What should be done differently? What should we learn for the next project? Did we make a Good Team? As the project leader, you shouldn't be talking too much, get the questions out there and wait to see what everyone says (cake helps here).

Take everything that's said and put it into some sort of mini-report or notes, and send this out to everyone who was involved. Success comes from building on past experiences, and there's no better way to improve your next project than by discussing the last one.

Fixing failure: When things go wrong

Admit to mistakes

When I started out in industry I was told a simple rule: "You'll make mistakes. We expect that. All we ask is that you don't make the same mistake twice." When you do something wrong (which you will), admit to it, tell your boss that something went wrong and give an overview of what it is. At the same time, *tell them what you are doing to fix it*. Even if your approach is completely wrong, you need to be thinking about the problem and methods of solving it. Ask for help here – is your approach correct? What else could you do? Then take this advice and fix the mistake. Once you've solved it, write down your mistake, what you should have done, and the solution you ended up taking. You will thus (hopefully) avoid making the same mistake again, and if you do screw up twice, now you know the solution.

The most important part in all of this is not to avoid blame, whether it be via blaming other people or hiding away and sending everything in an email just before you leave for the weekend. It's tempting, especially when it's a major screw-up, but getting a reputation as someone who dodges responsibility will basically kill your future career.

Deal with it

Stuff goes wrong, and things will be harder than you think. There'll be chaos and drama and lost batches and moments where you need to figure out just what is going on before everything falls into chaos. You'll be stressed and wish that you could just walk away and leave it all behind. Don't. Take a deep breath. Deal with it. Avoiding the problem will always make it worse, running away from the office while giggling madly about freedom is usually considered a bad career move. One of the reasons you've been hired is because of your skill at problem solving (it's a major advantage of a life-science background) and so your manager will be expecting you to solve the problem. So get stuck in, figure it out, deal with the problem. Nothing will push you onto a fast career track quite like being known as a problem solver. Then you'll get bigger, more stressful problems to solve. Life's funny like that.

Conflict and clashing priorities

Conflict is one of those subjects that can fill up hundreds of books, and indeed has. Conflict *is* something that will come up during your professional career, whether it be personal conflicts or conflicts between priorities and goals. We're just going to cover the basics here, because this is a field where the basic approach will suffice for the majority of your needs in the first year or two. If you're having serious troubles, then it's time to look for some more detailed advice. The first section will cover how you can deal with clashes between the priorities of you, your boss, and your other co-workers. The second will focus on conflicts which occur when a minor disagreement between co-workers flares up into arguments and hatred.

Clashing Priorities

One of the most common causes of 'work related' problems you will encounter is that of clashing priorities – you would like QA to finish reviewing a vital document today, but QA would like to finish a deviation report first. Both of these priorities are important, but your top priority (the review) and their top priority (the report) are at cross-purposes and cannot be performed at the same time. This is amazingly common when dealing with the real world (enough to be a common interview question), and if not solved can lead to entire projects being derailed. How do you fix clashing priorities? It usually comes down to understanding, compromise, scheduling, a good chunk of discussion, and (if all else fails) management.

First comes understanding. Talk to each other and determine how your respective priorities stack up. What tasks need to be completed by each side of the disagreement? How important are they? How urgent? Remember that there is a difference between important and urgent, urgent but unimportant tasks are a massive time-waster for all involved. Which task will have a greater effect on the company or your individual careers? Which has the higher priority? In case of doubt, refer this last question to your manager or the group project manager.

Next, compromise. Based on what both of you have to do, work out a compromise schedule in which both tasks will be completed. If one is obviously more important than the other then it will obviously need to be done first, but remember that you can always make partial compromises by offering to help smooth other parts of the workload, rearrange schedules, or even just bribe them with coffee and beer. As in all negotiations, the more variables that you can work with the more likely it is that both of you will come away satisfied.

Lastly, don't be afraid to ask your manager for advice or a ruling. They will normally have a better idea of which task is actually more important for the company. Your manager can either directly state what each of you should do (if you are in the same group) or speak to your counterparts' manager directly. Never go directly to the manager of the person you are clashing with, this will simply seem arrogant and unprofessional. Once a ruling has come down then accept it – if their task was judged to be more important, tough luck.

Always remember that you need to keep working with each other after this (possibly for many years to come). Strive to be calm, rational, and ready to compromise – this will save you a lot of frustration in the long run.

Personal Conflict
As you would expect, working together with other people means that there is the chance for conflicts to arise. This can be from minor reasons (who didn't refill the coffee jug?) through to major things (who didn't complete their part of the project?) and very often comes up because people have different priorities on their time or different approaches to doing their work. Regardless of the initiating factor you are going to have to deal with the conflict –

leaving it to fester will simply cause major problems down the line.

First step is to take a deep breath and think calmly about what is happening – what are you two saying to each other, what's the underlying cause? People work at a number of different levels, starting with the obvious things that they can observe and then working down to less obvious things such as internal interpretation of observations, feelings induced by those interpretations, the way those feelings and interpretations clash with core values, all sorts of things. Generally a conflict situation is going to occur because of clashes between these underlying levels – this is why so many long-held arguments seem strange to people on the outside, because they can only see the surface layer. This means that if you are trying to *solve* a conflict, you need to try and understand the underlying cause of everybody's actions – don't just look at what they're doing, think about why that might be happening.

The second step is then to try and discuss the conflict. Sounds easy, right? It's not – though your approach can make a big difference to your chances of success. You'll read a lot about using collaborative and inclusive statements when working through personal conflicts, and to be honest these tend to work fairly well once you get past the slightly awkward feeling of prefacing all your comments with 'I feel'. If you're not a huge fan of this, then the best way to deal with conflicts is usually to calmly describe your side of the event with a clear separation between what you *observed* and what you *interpreted*. Essentially you want to state your observation, describe your interpretation of that observation, and then describe the feelings that interpretation invoked.

What does that actually mean in practice? Here's an example: "I saw you playing on the phone during my presentation last week (observation). I considered that to be a sign that you weren't interested in my work (interpretation). That lack of interest offended me (associated feelings)." Simple, right? Naturally in actual practice this will be a longer speech than a three-sentence example, but the basic structure should allow you to keep the discussion on a professional level.

You'll want to have this kind of discussion in a quiet room somewhere, just the two of you. Try to keep it professional – don't make things personal, don't insult the other person, don't be sarcastic (even if you're normally sarcastic, this just makes things worse), don't say things like "why didn't you say this before?" (this *also* makes things worse). Just be polite and calm, and try to stay that way even when you're both discussing the things that annoy you about the other. Usually the best approach is to get all of these problems and talking points out in the open *before* you start looking at ways to solve them or make compromises. This stops you from missing something and then bringing it up later, ruining all of the work done so far.

Once this is done you'll move into step three: the negotiation or discussion phase. Spend some time beforehand thinking about what you're annoyed about and what sort of actions you want from the other person. What are you willing to overlook? What are your non-negotiables? How could you both change your actions so that you are happy (or at least not upset) with the final outcome? The whole idea of 'win-win' is nice in principle but rarely achievable in practice – thus it's important to think about what you want, what they want, and what you're both willing to compromise on. This is the basis for solving conflicts in almost all areas of life – take the chance to get some practice.

So you've both got your viewpoints out in the open, discussed what you need to do, and agreed on an approach. Right? Now it's time to pull it all together and restate, again, just what actions you're both going to take. This is like any other meeting – if you don't come out with a clear set of goals afterwards then it was just a waste of time. Hopefully your agreed actions help out and the situation will return to normal. If you can't reach an agreement, or the conflict stays around afterwards, then it's time to start talking to your manager.

When should you involve your manager? There are different approaches here, depending on how much of a micromanager they are, but you should at least try to work things out together before escalating. A good rule of thumb is that while you are still talking with each other, you can solve the problem by yourselves. Once the conflict becomes more important than the issue, which you'll first notice as people start building coalitions to defend their side, then you'll need your manager to solve it. And when you get to the point where it's no longer about the conflict and more about simply screwing over the other person, then resolving the problem starts to require legal action and people getting fired. Try not to get this far.

Overworked?

No matter how organised you are, you're going to have times when there is simply too much to do and not enough time. You'll be running around like a madman dealing with six deviations and a couple of change evaluations, then a new project will pop up. This is even worse at the start of your career because you won't be certain whether you *should* be so stressed or if you are just being a whingy academic who can't cope with the industry pace.

Partly this is true – industry jobs are a lot faster-paced than academic ones and emergencies will occur far more often than during your PhD. In general you should expect to be working solidly through the entire day, and you'll often find that you'll be exhausted when you get home. As long as you can keep up with it all, then you're going well. When it gets too much though, and you're having trouble getting your primary jobs done... well, then it's getting dangerous for both your health and your career. It's time to start asking for help.

As with any other problem that you can't solve by yourself, the next step is to talk to your manager. Explain the problem calmly, with details about the different projects you're working on and the time you need for each. Mention what you've done to try and fix the overwork problem, and ask for their advice. Generally your manager will care about your workload, if for no other reason than that your success will affect their success. More importantly, they've been doing this for a long time and have experienced this situation before.

Together you should be able to think up some approaches which you can use to deal with the situation. Make sure you take notes of your discussion and follow-up on any specific instructions that you're given (particularly when it comes to passing work to other people or delaying deadlines). You can also take this chance to ask for some more general tips on dealing with workload, particularly regarding task prioritisation – which of your typical tasks do they consider most important, and which least?

Beyond the first half year: Developing your career

You make your own success. This is true in academia, it is extremely true in industry. If you want to climb the career ladder in your company or field, you need to first sit down and realise that everything is up to you. Your drive, your dedication, your sheer bloody-mindedness. You.

Alright, sounds good, but what does that actually mean? It means that you need to have a plan for where you'll be going in the near and distant future. This can be a very nebulous plan, (very few people can accurately pick out their career path five or ten years down the track), but you should at least have an idea of where you want to go next.

No idea? First off, what do you enjoy? Specialised skills, varied challenges, management role, development, quality assurance? There's a huge range of pharmaceutical jobs out there, and people who have entered the field at one firm are usually quite successful at switching between roles. Talk to the people in your company and find out what they do, see if it is the sort of thing you would enjoy.

Next step – is it possible? How long do people usually stay in your position before moving onwards, upwards, or outwards? Small but growing companies tend to have faster upward mobility (because talent has a chance to shine) but larger companies will have more options to switch between. What sort of firm are you working in? Does it match your preferences? How does it match up to the greater pharmaceutical field? This is where that broader reading we told you to do before comes into play.

Once you've a vague idea of where you want to go, then it's time to... you guessed it, *plan*! What skills do you need for the target role? What contacts? Where can you learn or meet them, respectively? Not only does this kind of information make you better in your current role, it gives you a head start on the way to the future position too. Success in knowledge fields like pharma depends on, well, knowledge – what and who you know, and what you do with that knowledge.

Make the opportunity to excel

If you're ambitious, then you're likely looking to take charge of a major project – something that will let you show your managers and co-workers just how good you actually are. But you've just spent the first half of the year working on small things and simplistic projects, mostly because you're new and still learning. How do you make the jump over to more interesting work?

First, of course, you need to be competent (duh), but just as importantly you need to be able to *demonstrate* this to your manager. If you know what to do but no-one ever realises this, well, your career isn't going to go well. Second, you need to make it clear that you *want* the extra responsibility – very often no-one will realise this because you've been too shy to simply say it out loud. Say it. If there is a bit of work you really want to take on, go into a meeting with your manager and *ask for it*. Present a plan of action and a list of potential issues to show that you've really thought about your approach, ask for the project. Most of the time the discussion will end up with you in the project lead seat. Just make sure you finish it successfully, or the opportunity won't come again.

Learn to network

Who you know can make a huge influence on your overall career, because a wide collection of friends can boost your job performance as well as opening up a number of further job opportunities. Building a network of contacts is a vital part of career development and you'll find that the contacts you build in your first industry job will last for many years.

So how does it help? How do contacts improve job performance? Simple really – as you get to know different people, you will end up with contacts who are knowledgeable in a wide range of different fields (even if you only hang out with QA people, for example). This means that when you have a question, you'll know who you can call or write to ask for help – positions such as regulatory affairs are almost entirely dependent on knowing the right people to ask for answers. Knowing who to ask when a problem comes up will save you countless hours searching online and will improve your efficiency immensely.

From a career perspective, the majority of job opportunities which are out there are never listed on online portals or advertised by the company. Instead, they are often created by a company in response to a need which someone is able to fill – the potential employee drives the position, not the other way around. How do you find these jobs? Well, you need to know people, and people need to know you.

How do people get to know you, and vice versa? You need to get out there and talk to them. Go to conferences, work catch-ups, visit a trade-show, become part of a club in your area, update your LinkedIn profile – there are many different ways you can meet people. But you won't meet people sitting on your arse at home, so get on out there.

This can be a problem for some people, particularly because the word 'networking' tends to have a somewhat dodgy association. This association is mostly because the people we think of as 'networkers' are, well, the slightly slimy ones who are obviously only talking to you for their own gain. Don't want to be that person? The solution is simple: *actually be interested in whoever you are talking to.* Easy. If you are speaking with someone at a meeting or conference, don't spend the time thinking about how they can help you. Instead think about how you can help them – do you know someone or something that might help their problem? Could you answer a question or introduce them to someone who knows a lot about the field? Have you seen an interesting article which they might want to be aware of? Do the introduction, answer the question, forward the article. If you help someone out first then they will usually help you at some stage in the future when you have the problem. Networking and maintaining a network is all about helping each other out, not about how you can 'extract value' from the relationship.

Specialise in one area, or specialise in generalising

What am I talking about? There are two general routes to success in a company environment. One of these involves specialising – being known for doing one thing much, much better than other people. Often this is something you would never think of before you begin – becoming an expert in submitting manufacturing process changes to the Japanese regulatory authorities, to take an example I know of. Specialists are very useful for companies which need that level of knowledge, and due to this rarity can command a very high price – a secure job and a good salary for full-time employees, a stream of projects for freelancers. This is the big fish in a small pond approach (start-ups tend to call it a 'niche') and is the main path most employees follow during their careers.

The other route to success involves being known as someone who is not a specialist in any one field, but who is an expert at leading teams of specialists to achieve results. This is the manager or project manager career path, and it requires both a good grasp of the technicalities of your field (because otherwise you'll never understand the problem), an ability to organise (obviously) and the personnel skills required to lead. This is a tricky combination, thus people who are able to come in and solve problems with a group of wildly disparate experts are sought after in every branch of the pharmaceutical industry (and beyond).

Regardless of which path you follow, gaining this kind of expertise takes effort and practice. You can often get to the point of being competent within a year of starting your first pharma job, you'll be very competent indeed within three years. Becoming an expert requires deliberately setting out to find those small things which you can do to push yourself beyond everyone else. Not sure what those are? Talk to people in the field, ask for their tips and tricks, experiment with your approach to your tasks, always try to learn something.

Hold on – I'm a manager?

It's unlikely that you'll find yourself in a team leader role coming directly out of academia, however you have a good chance of being promoted into one of these roles within a few years if you are good enough. Even for those who aren't officially managers, many tasks within the pharmaceutical world are performed as part of ad-hoc teams – teams with no official reporting relationship but nonetheless contain one person who is needed to organise the project. This sort of role is often given to people within their first year and thus you need to know how to manage and how to lead in order to move your career forward.

So how do you lead people when you're at the same level in the company as they are? Or in a completely different department, but part of your wider project group? This is where you need to have the confidence and respect of the people you are co-ordinating – and this is something that is built over time.

First, you need to show that you are actually competent enough to do your current work, let alone guide others. Are you able to complete your assigned tasks and projects quickly and reliably? With a minimum of whinging and complaining? And often going a little bit beyond what is expected of you? Great! People *will* notice your competence, and this is the first step in becoming a manager.

Second, you need to demonstrate that you can plan out projects and deal with setbacks. We've filled another section (pg. 73) with some useful information on project planning, use these skills to plan out your larger work. Keep your manager informed of what you are doing and don't be afraid to show your co-workers how you keep track of everything. Most pharma firms are more chaotic than you would expect as a beginner and you will rapidly develop a reputation as the 'planning guy'.

Third, learn to make decisions. It is very, very easy to fall into the fear of saying the wrong thing or making a decision that will lead to non-optimal outcomes. You need to fight against the tendency to continually second-guess your thoughts or to constantly seek the opinions of others. Look at the information, ask for more if necessary, and then make a decision. There is nothing wrong with asking for help from colleagues or managers, indeed you should do this for topics you are unclear or unconfident about. But in the end, nothing of importance can be done without someone making a decision. That someone is you.

Fourth, learn to share the credit. It is sometimes tempting to take the credit for projects which have been completed, especially if you feel that you did the majority of the work. But that success was depending on all the help you got from other people – even small things which you may not think of as being that important. Nothing irritates a team more than the leader taking all the credit and very few things will make them less likely to work with you in future. You'll be a successful manager and leader when you realise that your success is directly related to how well your team performs. So make them look good, point out their notable successes to managers, share the credit when the project goes well.

Fifth, let people think. This is the other side of the credit coin – people need to earn the credit that they are given, and that means they need to think for themselves. Don't become a micromanager, constantly telling people how they should go about doing a task in excruciating detail. Instead, acknowledge that anyone working with you is probably fairly smart and so can figure out a lot of these things by themselves. Make sure everyone knows the final goal and what they need to achieve to get the team to that point. Then let them figure it out. This doesn't mean you should ignore them – always keep in touch and ask questions about how it is going, but your job is to *guide* their efforts towards success rather than doing the thinking for them.

You may have noticed that the advice in the last few paragraphs subtly shifted from advice for you as a *person* to advice for you as a *leader*. Here, as in real life, there is rarely a moment where you are told 'right, now you're responsible, have fun'. Instead it is a succession of steadily-increasing responsibilities, normally involving being given a task (e.g. write this report) and an ad hoc team (e.g. ask Bill and Diane for help with data collection). Seems simple? Well, now you have a project, people to co-ordinate…and suddenly you're a part-time manager. Be alert for these moments, because it is very easy to miss a career-boosting opportunity while thinking that it is just another stupid report to be written.

Moving on

You won't stay at the same job for your entire career, which means that at some stage you have to be prepared to leave. This may be because you've found an even better opportunity elsewhere, because you're being promoted upwards within the company, or because you don't particularly like your current position.

The move into pharma industry is a big one with a lot of sudden changes, and it is perfectly ok to decide after a while that this job is simply not ok for you. This might be because you dislike the work being done, the processes in place, the people you work with, the ones you work for – there are a multitude of reasons why you may want to leave. Regardless of the reason, the time you spend in this first job will make your CV look much better (the *second* job in industry is much easier to get than the first one) and will have given you a lot of experience in how a company works together. So it is never time wasted, but similarly you shouldn't wait around for months hoping that it will get better. Be honest with yourself – what could change that would make you stay? Would it actually be different, enough to make a change to your current level of happiness?

If the decision has been made, then you need to leave like a professional. Give the right amount of notice to your boss, then HR, then your colleagues – the industry standard is two weeks but you should check your contract to see if a longer period is required. Finish up your remaining work and document the projects and assignments that you will be leaving unfinished – your co-workers will love not having to trawl through your old files. Similarly, hold 'hand-over' meetings with everyone who will be taking over your work, get them up to speed with the project and help answer any questions they have.

There's normally an exit interview with HR or management when you leave. Be honest but clever in your answers to their questions – don't spend the time insulting your co-workers. The pharma world is surprisingly small, people will end up hearing about the time you screamed at your old boss before storming out the door – and they'll remember it when you come to the next interview with them too. Similarly, don't send the 'nasty farewell email'. You know which one, the vicious email listing (in careful detail) all of the reasons why everyone is a moron, why management has no idea, and why a *real* company would have better coffee in the break room. This is never a good idea (seriously, never), so avoid the temptation.

Mysterious jobs: positions in pharma

The pharmaceutical industry is significantly more complex than academia. It is not enough to simply make a pharmaceutical, you need to have people verifying the quality, registering processes with health authorities, finding customers, researching improvements – a vast number of jobs which simply don't exist in the basic-research system. Because of this many people coming from a university background have absolutely no idea what is going on – confused by strange titles such as clinical research associate or quality assurance manager. What do they do? Will I enjoy the job?

To help answer this question, this section of the book will focus on the typical 'entry-level' job descriptions which you will see on job boards or in advertisements. There are many, many more jobs out there, naturally, but these are some of the most common ones which you will be able to reach coming out of an academic/life-science background.

Many of these roles are completely different to the laboratory environment which is prevalent in academia (you will never touch a pipette in regulatory affairs, for example). Thus these roles have been ordered based on the highly technical term known as 'scienceness' – how similar is the role to what you would be doing within an academic environment? Those who are still looking for their ideal job may find this useful in determining where they should focus their applications, those who have recently started can see where they fall on the scale. In all cases it is helpful to know what the other people in your company actually *do* all day.

Typical entry roles within the pharmaceutical industry	
Scienceness (similarity to academia)	**Role**
High	Scientists and technical/research assistants (pg. 96)
	Bioinformatician (pg. 97)
	Laboratory head (pg. 98)

	Validation expert (pg. 99)
	Quality manager (pg. 100)
	Product manager (pg. 101)
	Regulatory affairs managers (pg. 102)
	Medical writer (pg. 103)
	Project manager (pg. 104)
	Clinical research associate (pg. 106)
	Pharmacovigilance officer (pg. 107)
	Medical science liaison (pg. 107)
	Sales and product experts (pg. 108)
Low	Marketing manager (pg. 109)

Scientists and technical/research assistants

Obsessed with paperwork as it seems to be, the core of the pharmaceutical industry is still those who work in the laboratory – scientists and technical assistants. The boundary between the two is fluid and varies from company to company, but a good rule of thumb is that scientists are expected to do more independent research while technical/research assistants are expected to perform more equipment-specific and support work.

Unlike academia, industry research is very focused on achieving something tangible and *saleable* – this can be a promising drug candidate, a new technology, a process improvement, etc. etc. This means that research projects will be ruthlessly cut if they do not appear to be making progress (or even if the market conditions have changed), and this in turn means that industry scientists need a more relaxed attitude than their academic counterparts. In other words: don't get too upset if your favourite candidate is axed, that's just how it goes.

Another difference is the more extensive set of rules and regulations which surround industry research. There will be **standard operating procedures** (SOPs) for almost every piece of equipment or experiment you have access to; most labs now run under good laboratory practice (GLP) or good development practice (GDevP) and thus have rules regarding how you do things such as saving data or signing lab-books. There is thus less flexibility than the equivalent academic lab – your goals will be set in conjunction with the lab head and blue-sky independent research is not particularly welcome.

A PhD is by no means required to work in a pharmaceutical laboratory, and indeed the company will often take people directly after their university degree. A PhD is almost always required for a scientist role, laboratory experience is very, very helpful for those after a technical assistant role. Naturally the lab experience should be with similar equipment and techniques, though HR may ignore this if they like you enough.

Scientist/technical assistant positions offer similar advantages to academic research, albeit with a requirement for more focus and flexibility than otherwise. A technical assistant role is a good entry point for those without interest in doing a PhD, it pays fairly well, provides industry experience, and often provides the opportunity to do a PhD within the company should you so desire. Similarly, those who want to continue research but want more structure than academia will enjoy the scientist role. Both allow upward mobility, but progress may be limited by the comparative lack of leadership and management skills required in the position.

Bioinformatician

Computers are involved in basically everything, and so it's no surprise that they are a huge part of pharmaceutical development as well. The ridiculous amounts of data produced during research (particularly when genomic or metabolomics testing gets involved) means that people who are able to work with this kind of data are treasured. Bioinformatics experts are responsible for putting together the programs and databases which allow valid results to be pulled out of a giant pile of biological data – think of them as the big data experts of the medical research world.

These roles are usually focused in the early stages of pharmaceutical development, doing tasks such as structural analysis of target proteins, hunting for biomarkers in patient data, or bringing disparate data together into a comprehensive model. People are usually hired directly after a PhD in a similar role to ensure that they have the required knowledge – skills which are further looked for include analytical and logical thinking and a comfort with mathematical processes.

Bioinformatics experts are usually well paid, a consequence of their comparative rarity and importance. Similarly the worldwide demand for these skills means that they can easily switch companies or even industries as desired – bioinformatics is a very good entry to a number of positions. However, the role usually doesn't include management-related activities, which means that those who are interested in leading a group will need to stretch themselves further than the job requires.

Laboratory head

Someone has to run the laboratory, and that someone is the lab head – the industry equivalent to your academic supervisor. As in academia, they are responsible for keeping everyone on track, ensuring the required results come out, and keeping everything within budget. Unlike academia, the focus is no longer on publications – instead industry labs focus on results for the company, with different areas depending on their specialisation. These can occur at the start of the entire process (development labs must identify a certain number of lead compounds per year) to the end (quality control labs will need to check drug product batches after manufacture) and at many stages in between.

Regardless of specialisation, lab heads will be organisers and managers – they will not perform the experiments themselves but will be involved in interpretation and report writing. As with all management positions, lab heads need to understand that their success is directly related to the success of their team. They need to keep the long-term goals in mind while assigning short-term goals to their team. This is particularly important in the often-frustrating world of development – lab heads need to keep motivation up and help find ways around the daily roadblocks.

The lab head role is a complex one requiring scientific knowledge, an understanding of commercial processes, organisational skills and leadership ability. They need to be responsible for training employees on the equipment and making sure that everything is performed according to the relevant SOPs (as well as good development/laboratory practice where relevant). Despite all the paperwork, the main skills needed revolve around team leadership and management. These roles usually require a completed PhD and often a term as a postdoc, making them one of the more difficult options for those entering industry for the first time.

Validation expert

A standard requirement of good manufacturing practice is that processes need to be **validated.** Process validation is a formal set of steps by which the process is shown to work consistently well, leading to a final result or product of sufficient quality. Validation is performed when making new processes (e.g. starting manufacture of a new drug), when making changes to old processes (e.g. new filters on the sterile line) or as a yearly check (e.g. do our sterilisation methods still work?). *Qualification* is similar to *validation*, albeit it with a focus on equipment and things rather than processes. The employee in charge of this process has many names, but they are most often known as the validation expert, validation manager, or validation engineer.

The job of the validation expert is to plan out, run, and summarise the results of process validation testing. The beginning of this involves determining which tests will be performed and what results will need to be obtained to be considered 'success' – these will be written up in the appropriate process validation protocol. As this kind of planning requires a good degree of technical knowledge, validation experts are usually drawn from those with experience in the field. Testing will be performed according to this written protocol, and once tested the expert will write up the associated validation report. This is considered a very important GMP-related document and often used for regulatory filings, as such there will be a lot of pressure from almost everyone to get it right.

Validation or qualification experts need a lot of expertise in their chosen field, which limits entry into this position for beginners. However, those with a good background in biotech studies combined with proven analytical thinking skills may be able to work their way into a very interesting role.

Quality manager

You will end up hearing the word 'quality' a lot when working in pharma, and the main people responsible for this word are quality managers, usually divided into quality assurance and quality control. These roles involve keeping an overview of the general quality level of the product, process, and raw materials, stepping in to stop things when quality problems start to occur. Their overall goal is to keep the product up to the required standards and improve it whenever possible.

This means keeping track of testing results and required specifications, calculating possible trends in quality which may lead to problems in the future, and keeping an eye out that everything is performed according to the respective GxP guidelines. Quality managers will be involved in health authority inspections and will often take the lead during inspections by the company of other suppliers or internal processes. This is, unsurprisingly, a fairly stressful time and so quality managers shouldn't be surprised to pull very long weeks when this happens.

When something does go wrong, quality managers also take the lead in deviation investigations and reporting on the cause of the problem. This can be highly frustrating or entertaining, depending on your enjoyment of problem-solving and investigational tasks. It can also be extremely stressful when the root cause of a deviation needs to be determined within a short period of time (particularly when it is required prior to batch release – time is money when the drug is already sitting on the shelf).

The variety of tasks make the position an 'intermediary' role, interacting with people from many different branches, and thus requires a good level of communication skills. However the most important talent is the ability to stand your ground in the face of pressure. Many people will try to push quality managers to quickly release batches, approve documents, sign off on a deviation, etc. A good quality manager will need a certain degree of stubbornness and the willingness to say 'no' until the legal requirements have been fulfilled. Quality is a common entry field for those entering industry and is important enough that you will always be able to get a job – career safety is almost guaranteed.

Product manager

A product manager is, well, in charge of a product – think of a particular pharmaceutical or diagnostic machine. They have the responsibility to bring the product to success across the entirety of its life-cycle – from development, during entrance to the market and then throughout the sales lifetime. As the go-to expert for the product they usually spend a lot of their time co-ordinating activities between and answering questions from many different departments, in particular marketing, development, production and sales. As you would expect, this requires good planning skills combined with conflict-management experience.

A major part of a product manager's role focuses on the product launch, the point at which it enters the market and can be bought by customers. There are marketing strategies to be discussed, documents for the sales workers to review, comments to make and a lot of questions to answer. As most successful product managers were also present during the development phase, they have a deep level of knowledge about the product which can help suggest approaches when problems pop up.

The other side of product management involves lifecycle planning – deciding when updates to the product should come onto the market, replacing obsolete versions or being sold alongside. This requires a lot of communication between marketing (who determine what the customers actually want) and development (who determine what can actually be done). Often new ideas for product specifications or offerings will come from conversations with customers, and these can lead to major changes in the product over time.

Product managers need scientific knowledge to understand the intricacies of their product, but they also need a broader knowledge of commercial practices to be able to analyse market sizes and survey feedback. The heavy reliance on knowledge means that product manager positions are a good goal for those interested in a technical but non-lab-related role with flexible tasks and a good bit of responsibility.

Regulatory affairs managers

Regulatory affairs managers are responsible for getting approval from regulatory bodies for medications, clinical trials, and changes to approved processes. These departments are known as health authorities and control drug approvals and submissions – think of the US Food and Drug Administration (FDA). The legal right to sell a drug relies on the Health Authority agreeing with the company's assessment of its safety and efficacy – putting together this persuasive argument is the job of regulatory affairs managers.

This is done via the **dossier**, a vast document split into numerous sections which covers every stage of the past development process and the future plans. As you would expect given its importance, working on a product's dossier takes up a lot of time. Whether it's putting together the initial application or making updates to a previously-approved one, a regulatory career will revolve around the dossier. The dossier is derived from source documents prepared by other departments within the firm. Others within the company will be doing protein analysis, clinical studies, purity checks – this is not the job of regulatory affairs. Instead they take the studies and reports from these people and use that as a basis for their own writing. Experience dealing with scientific data and methods remains vital, even though regulatory does not do their own scientific work.

Regulatory managers are called upon to give input to ongoing studies and proposed changes to manufacturing processes. Pharmaceutical companies are constantly modify production methods to optimise for cost and yield. Many of these changes will need permission from the Health Authorities, and it will be up to regulatory affairs to say how much effort this will be. Similarly, their advice will be needed when it comes to planning these studies and changes. What will be needed to get approval for your drug? What kind of studies (be they lab work or clinical) will need to be in the final submission? These are questions which need to be answered throughout the drug's lifecycle – and this is where the regulatory affairs team comes in.

The tasks performed by regulatory are extremely variable and differ widely depending on what exact role they are playing – roles which can change from day to day. At the most basic level, regulatory affairs managers act as *traders in information*. They stand at the midpoint between a vast variety of departments, experts and regulators and need to keep information flowing between each and every one of them. Emails, reports, meetings, phone calls, the regulatory affairs job involves keeping people up to date and in the loop. Most regulatory managers will be juggling multiple projects at any one time, plus various meetings and whatever emergency has come up this time. They need the skills to plan both in the short term and the long term and then, as you would expect from the title, manage those projects. But it's not 'management' in the sense of having direct reports who do the tasks you assign them – instead it's managing people without actually having any formal authority over them. You can't give orders, you'll have to persuade, wheedle, nag, bargain, compromise and trade your way to your goals. Because of this interpersonal skills are one of the most sought-after attributes by those looking to hire new regulatory managers.

Medical writer

A medical writer is employed by the pharmaceutical company to create documents for various audiences, usually with a focus on regulatory authorities, healthcare professionals or the general public. Being able to write well is a surprisingly rare talent, the majority of internal pharma documents are obtuse, highly repetitive, and highly repetitive in their repetition. As such those who can take complex concepts and articulate them clearly are very valuable to the company.

Medical writers will often find themselves preparing documents to educate healthcare professionals – think of journal articles, sales literature, pamphlets and presentations. These are intended to persuade readers of the advantages of the pharmaceutical and thus medical writing is often considered a part of the overall marketing campaign for new or current drugs. The other side of medical writing involves preparing documents for regulatory submissions. Although the dossier preparation will be performed by regulatory affairs, medical writers will be called upon to prepare clinical study protocols and reports, investigator brochures and other documents required during the course of a clinical trial.

Although larger firms will have their own group of medical writers, smaller companies will usually outsource the work to specialised groups or individual contractors. As such medical writing is a field in which it is very possible to be a successful freelancer rather than a salaried employee. Regardless of employment status, medical writers will need persuasive writing skills and the ability to bring clarity to complex themes.

Project manager

'Project manager' is a fairly general term, and indeed it is a job which can be found in pretty much every field. Project managers are responsible for organising **projects**, tasks with defined goals, beginnings, and ends. These are often special events which occur outside the normal daily routine – think of the effort required to run a new clinical trial or implement a new production line. Both of these have defined goals and will have a set period of time set aside in which they can be done – once complete, all people involved will move on to other work.

Project managers do not do the actual work themselves, but are instead responsible for managing everyone else's efforts. This involves a lot of planning and estimating at the start, monitoring during the implementation phase, and a whole lot of organising throughout. Time is almost always the limiting factor in pharma projects, so they are also directly involved in making *realistic* timelines and then ensuring everyone follows them.

The project manager is expected to have a status overview at all times and should be actively heading off problems which may be about to occur. Most projects run into delays or problems so project managers need to be flexible and realistic enough to change tasks around when needed – as well as cheerful enough to encourage the team through the difficulty. As they usually work with inter-departmental teams without direct reporting lines, project managers must be managers without giving orders – this in turn requires good leadership talents.

Once finished, the project manager then wraps up everything in a nice report, complete with recommendations for future work and lessons learned from this one, ensures the deliverables have been delivered, and then moves onto the next project. At least, in theory – realistically most project managers will have multiple projects going on at once and so will simply shift their focus to the next one.

The role of project manager is a varied and exciting one. It will bring you into contact with many different projects and has the advantage of having a defined 'success' condition which will appeal to those who like to tick off accomplishments. Those interested in the field require excellent organisation and time management skills, as well as the ability to set priorities for those they are organising – you need to know when a task is simply not worth spending time on. Those who excel in project management will find a long career ahead of them, and one which can easily be switched between industries as needed.

Clinical research associate

A Clinical Research Associate (CRA) job is a typical starting position for people entering the pharmaceutical industry. Their job revolves around organising and monitoring clinical studies. You'll normally be working for a contract research organisation or large pharmaceutical firm, with the exact requirements changing from position to position.

Before the study begins CRAs will be needed to help recruit doctors and medical locations into the study. The clinical study itself needs to be planned and there needs to be documented evidence that the doctor understands the regulatory requirements. Clinical trials need to be conducted according to **Good Clinical Practice** (GCP), a series of rules and guidelines which cover things such as requiring informed consent from patients and getting signatures on documents saying that they fully understand the risks. They also need to ensure that the information being developed is properly anonymised prior to use. But wait, there's more! CRAs also perform feasibility analysis (which facilities would be the best suited to this clinical study?), pre-study visits (a formal check-and-sign-off of the proposed site), work closely with regulatory affairs (to prepare documents for the drug submission), and keep the clinical study plan up to date.

Once the study has begun, the CRA still has work to do. They need to monitor the study itself, ensuring that it is being performed according to GCP and the other agreements made during the planning phase. They solve problems as they pop up and keep all of the different parties informed of progress.

As a general rule, the job will be very variable. A CRA doesn't deal with patients themselves, this is the role of the doctor, but they can be considered the middle-point between the trial doctors and the study sponsor. CRA work is a combination of desk work and facility visits, which means that a willingness to travel is also a necessity, and they spend a lot of time in meetings and having phone calls – so a CRA needs patience and people skills to sort problems out without bruising too many egos.

Pharmacovigilance officer

Pharmacovigilance (PV) is a vital part of ensuring that a drug is safe to use, revolving as it does around collecting information on adverse events and other failures in drug safety or efficacy. The common entry point to PV is the position known as pharmacovigilance officer or drug safety associate. This is a case-processing role, in that it involves taking reports from around the world and then entering this information into a common database, ready to be evaluated and assessed by dedicated risk management teams. PV officers are also required to follow-up on reports to obtain further information and then write the case narrative from this information.

Beyond this PV officers will be involved in writing the regulatory reports of safety events which will be sent to the health authorities, will screen medical literature to identify potential adverse events, and will be involved in the review of clinical trial protocols and reports.

Career progression from this point usually goes into management roles or the specialised technical roles, including risk management and epidemiology. Progression within the pharmacovigilance field can be difficult thanks to the high level of competition for higher positions and the requirement for specialised skills and training which are difficult for early-stage employees to gain. As such it is often easier for employees in smaller firms to gain the broad experience needed to move up the ladder than those in large pharmaceutical firms.

Medical Science Liaison

A medical science liaison (MSL) acts as the intermediary between the company and physicians or scientists – in particular those doing research in their field of interest. An MSL has a scientific background (they almost always have a doctorate of some form) and will usually specialise in a specific therapeutic area.

Medical science liaisons are considered to be experts in their field and with their specialty products of interest – they assist internal colleagues when needed as well as consulting with external healthcare providers. As with sales representatives, the MSL position is a field-based role involving interaction with physicians in the field of interest. Unlike sales representatives, MSLs build relationships with leading physicians and other key opinion leaders at major academic institutions or clinics. These relationships are considered more 'peer-peer' than that of sales representatives as both MSL and opinion leader are considered scientific experts.

Those with excellent communication skills, integrity, flexibility, and an interest in a career which merges science and marketing may want to look into the medical science liaison role. Gaining a position can be difficult due to the hefty requirements, although the number of open positions are increasing rapidly and the pay rates for the role are comparatively quite good.

Sales representatives and product experts

Although you probably started your career out in the lab, there's no reason why it has to stay in the lab – and there are a lot of careers looking for scientific skills. One common field here is that of sales representative and the associated product expert role, in which deep knowledge of the biotech or pharma product is required. The role essentially boils down to becoming an expert in the myriad intricacies of a particular product, and then using that knowledge to help potential and current customers.

People in these roles are usually involved in business-to-business (B2B) sales (for biotech companies) or business-to-healthcare provider sales (for pharmaceuticals). This is for the simple reason that the general public isn't all that interested in prescribing medications or owning a diagnostics device (or if they are, can't afford it). The positions are considered a 'customer facing' role and so there will almost always be training for new employees to ensure they know what they are doing and don't embarrass the company too much.

These roles are common for people entering the pharma industry for the first time, though it is an often-overlooked option. This is partly due to the travel requirements – those starting out will find themselves on the road quite often as they visit external clients. Product managers will usually find themselves doing site visits in the company of those working directly in sales, where product experts will be called upon to help answer customer questions. They will also find themselves working after-sales support, helping customers who have bought the product to use it to its full potential.

A specialised role within the field is that of the **key account managers**, who are dedicated to dealing with one or two major customers of the firm. These customers are considered to be large enough that losing them would seriously reduce company profits, and thus are worth the expense of a dedicated manager. Beyond this large companies tend to have complex contracts worked out over long negotiation sessions, which requires a more specialised level of knowledge than for run-of-the-mill customers.

These roles are suited the people with open, friendly and communicative personalities. They also require a good understanding of the commercial requirements of the industry (no ivory towers here), a willingness to travel when necessary, the ability to negotiate and persuade, and naturally an organised approach to the many different tasks you'll need to juggle. Pay is often based in large part on the sales you oversee, usually a percentage of the sales you make are provided as a bonus. This makes sales an area where your income is directly related to how well you perform, and one in which people who are competent can go very far, very fast.

Marketing manager

Companies that cannot sell their goods have a tendency to go bankrupt. Similarly, if no-one knows that the product exists, they aren't going to buy it. Solving this potentially quite fatal problem is where the marketing department comes in.

Marketing managers are responsible for bringing information on the product to those who should buy it: this can be in the form of talks, literature, conversations, exhibition booths, educational programs, fancy animated videos – if you can think of it, marketing has probably tried using it at some stage. But as the saying goes – half of every marketing budget is wasted, we just don't know which half. Marketing's job is to determine which areas bring the greatest return on their advertising dollar, and thus which should be focused on to help sell the product.

So how do they do that? It's an incredibly complex field (and far more detail than we'll go into here), but a major portion involves asking questions of those who use the product – the target market. Who are they, how much money do they have, can they afford to buy it? Does it match their needs and do we need to incorporate extra features? Do we have secondary groups buying which we aren't aiming for, and should we focus resources on them as well? This kind of information informs both the overall marketing strategy and the future development of the product.

Marketing managers are responsible for taking this information and then planning the overall marketing strategy, this will then be divided into a number of marketing activities which are either done in-house or outsourced. Specialised work (think of animated videos showing mode of action) are usually outsourced, though the marketing manager will still have the final responsibility for signing off on the work. As in all departments, this needs to be performed within budget and on schedule.

The jump into marketing is a big one. Communication skills tend to be the most important, followed by the ability to plan and a good dash of creativity. You need to be comfortable giving presentations, talented at explaining complex themes, and knowledgeable in the field. It is almost always a team-based role and so you will need to be both open to others and self-confident enough to argue your own beliefs. Much like sales, marketing is a field which is always needed in every industry – you will never have problems finding further jobs once you've begun.

A glossary of industry terminology

Term	Meaning
Active Air Monitoring	Using what is essentially a fancy vacuum cleaner to actively pull air across an agar plate, so as to determine how many microbes are floating around in your critical zone
Accelerated Study Conditions	Using higher temperature and humidity conditions during stability studies to force your product to degrade faster than usual.
Acceptance Limit	The point at which you can no longer accept a variable during manufacturing, and so have to discard the batch.
ADME	An acronym for Absorption, Distribution, Metabolism, and Excretion, it covers the processes by which a drug is taken up by the body, shuttled around, converted to other forms, and removed.
Adverse Event	The unwanted action of a drug – this can include side effects or cases where the drug simply doesn't work.
Airlock	Just like on a spaceship, this is a room with two doors designed to keep one side (the outside environment) separate from the other (the clean zone). There is usually a pressure-difference across the airlock to make sure microbes are blown away from the clean zone.
Alert level	The point at which your monitoring system says 'there *may* be a problem', and which leads to closer examination of the process.
Action Level	The point (higher than an alert level) at which there *is* a problem, and where you *have to* perform an investigation.

Active Pharmaceutical Ingredient (API)	The part of your final product which has an actual pharmaceutical effect
Aseptic Production	Producing your drug in an extremely sterile environment, as opposed to terminal sterilisation. This is the usual approach taken by biological drugs.
Aseptic Processing Facility	The part of the building where aseptic production is performed, separated from the outside environment by physical barriers, air filters, etc.
Bioburden	The number of microbes which are found on an item before sterilisation (or after, depending on your process)
Biological Indicator	A group of test microbes which are placed inside the equipment while testing the sterilisation process – if the sterilisation has worked, these microbes should also be dead.
Blow-Fill-Seal (BFS)	A manufacturing technique where plastic containers are extruded, blown into shape, filled with sterile liquids, and then sealed – all without exposure to the outside environment.
Bubble-Point Testing	Determining the presence of defects in a liquid filter by measuring the pressure needed to force bubbles through it.
Change Control	The process by which any changes to an approved process are evaluated and then implemented.
Corrective and Preventative Action (CAPA)	The outcome of a deviation investigation should be a set of actions that you will take to prevent the problem happening again – CAPAs.
Clean Zone	A subset of the aseptic facility, this is a region or room which has a set cleanliness level and which has been verified as achieving that level.

Clinical endpoint	Something which is being measured as the target outcome of a clinical trial – this can be highly specific (blood biomarkers) or general (patient survival)
Closure	Your drug is filled into a *container*, which is then sealed with a *closure* – think of lids, rubber stoppers, etc.
Colony forming unit (CFU)	After plating out a solution onto agar, a single microbe will grow into one small colony. This is a single CFU, and is usually considered to be 'one bacteria' (though it can be more in some species which 'stick' to each other)
Component	The term used to refer to the ingredients used to manufacture the final drug product – this can refer to the API, excipients, even the water for injection.
Contact Plate	Specially designed agar plates which can be directly pressed against surfaces to pick up any microbes which may be there.
Container	The sterile drug is filled into a container, such as a vial, a pre-filled syringe, etc. which is then sealed with a closure.
Continuing Medical Education	The requirement for healthcare professionals to continue learning after completing their degrees.
Critical Surface	Any surface which may directly contact the sterile product or container and thus one which needs to be carefully sterilised.
Critical Area / Critical Zone	The zone in which the sterile drug product and containers are exposed to the air, and thus the part with the highest requirements for cleanliness.
Deviation	Basically: When something goes wrong, requiring an investigation.

Disinfection	The process of killing everything which may be living on the surfaces of your clean room.
Dossier	A giant document which shows the regulatory authorities that the drug is safe and effective. It also acts as a contract between the company and the authority to state that the drug will be produced in exactly the agreed-upon manner. The life of regulatory affairs managers revolves around the dossier.
D-value	The time (in minutes) which a sterilisation process needs to reduce the number of microorganisms by 90% (i.e. 1-log).
Efficacy	How well the drug works.
Efficiency Testing (filters)	Testing a filter to see how effective it is at removing microbes.
Excipients	Everything which is present in the final drug product which is not the active pharmaceutical ingredient.
Empty Load	A sterilisation run without any contents to be sterilised, especially used for validation of the autoclave.
Endotoxin	A molecule such as lipopolysaccharides which are found in bacterial cell walls, and which lead to very dangerous immune reactions when introduced to the body.
Exclusivity	Time periods in which other companies are prevented from competing with a drug already on the market, this process is separate to that of patenting.
Executed Batch Record	The 'filled in' batch record, with all of the times, measurements, observations, etc. clearly recorded and signed off. This is *the* official record of the production process.

Generic	A copy of a pharmaceutical which can be produced once patent protection has expired.
Good Clinical Practice	A set of guidelines covering the 'best-practice' way to run a clinical trial.
Good Manufacturing Practice	A set of guidelines covering the 'best-practice' way to produce a pharmaceutical.
Heat Penetration Study	Testing the sterilisation process when loaded with typical items, to check whether tightly-packed or sealed objects are still sterilised correctly
HEPA Filter	'High efficiency particulate air' filter, a filter which removes 99.97% of all particles that are 0.3 μm and larger.
Hits	Compounds identified during drug screening which appear to have an effect on the chosen target.
Hold Time	A potential pause in the production process, it is not always required but provides time to fix any problems which may occur.
Indication	A disease or disease state which a drug has been given marketing approval to treat.
In-Process Control	Measurements of variables during production which are used to monitor and control the overall process.
Intended Study Conditions	Storage of a product at the intended storage temperature and humidity during a stability study – this is intended to demonstrate degradation when the drug is stored 'correctly'.
Intervention	The process of doing 'anything' which is not part of the normal production process within the aseptic zone.
Isolator	A large protective shell which protects the production line from the surrounding clean-room. It can be closed or open,

	depending on requirements, and has the same cleanliness as a critical zone.
Key Account Manager	With enough experience and talent, a sales expert can evolve (much like Pokémon) into a key account manager, ready to work with the most important clients of the company.
Key Opinion Leader	A leading figure within the healthcare industry, whose opinions (including those on pharmaceutical products) are able to influence their peers.
Lead compound	A compound which has shown promise in early drug development studies, and is now ready for more serious testing.
Leak Testing (filters)	In-place testing of the filter and its housing to ensure that it is working correctly.
Manufacturing Campaign	The production of a number of batches in sequence and within a given time period.
Mapping Study	A study to check if the sterilising equipment and process leads to equal temperature and pressure throughout the entire system.
Marketing Approval	The official confirmation that you can sell your pharmaceutical
Master Batch Record	The not-yet-filled-out record containing instructions for all steps in the production process.
Media Fill Study	A 'practice' run of your normal production/filling process using microbial growth media, to check whether everything comes out sterile.
Meeting Minutes	A summary of what was said at the meeting, who was there, and what was decided. Vital for ensuring that everyone actually follows up on the brilliant solutions thought up during the meeting itself.

Me-too Drug	A drug which is very, very similar to others which are already on the market, albeit with enough changes to avoid patent infringement.
Membrane Filter	A polymer membrane with tiny pores that block microbes/particles. Can be used for liquids or high-pressure gases.
Monograph	A description of the specifications and associated tests which should apply to a specific drug or raw material.
Off-label	Using a pharmaceutical to treat a disease for which it does not have marketing authorisation.
Passive Air Monitoring	Checking for the presence of airborne microbes by leaving an open agar plate out for a few hours.
Patent	The legal right to exclusive use of an invention in exchange for providing a detailed description which anyone can use after the patent expires.
Pharmacopeia	A giant book full of 'official' testing methods to use when identifying and ensuring the quality of various pharmaceuticals
Phase I-IV	The different stages of clinical trials, where the number of enrolled patients, importance, and costs increase dramatically with each stage.
Pre-clinical testing	Determining safety and efficacy of a candidate drug via animal trials.
Prescriber	Someone who is allowed to prescribe a pharmaceutical or other healthcare intervention for patients.
Process Characterisation	The act of performing numerous tests on your manufacturing process to see what variations lead to which changes in the final product or result.

Process Parameter	A measurable variable in the manufacturing process which has an effect on attributes of the final product.
Process Steps	The individual actions which a manufacturing process can be broken down into
Process Validation	Proving (and documenting) that your process is highly reproducible and leads to a high-quality final product.
Project	A set task with a defined start point, end point, and goal to achieve – this separates it from the usual daily work.
Pull Point	The time point at which a sample is removed from storage during a stability study and tested.
Qualification	Testing and documenting that the equipment is capable of acting as it should.
Quality-adjusted life-year	A way to compare healthcare interventions – a perfectly healthy year of life is 1 QALY, a year of being dead is 0, and various degrees of illness come somewhere in-between.
Quality Attribute	An attribute of the final product or intermediary which is related to the overall quality of the drug.
Regulatory Health Authority	Also known simply as Health Authorities, these are the government departments which oversee pharmaceutical approvals, sales, and changes. The most well-known of these is the US Food and Drug Administration (FDA), but every country will have their own health authority.
Release	The process by which a batch is declared to be ok, and set free to frolic joyfully across the rolling hills on the way to market.

Release Specification	The specifications which need to be met before a batch can be released.
Request for Information	The response a regulatory health authority sends when they are unhappy with something and would like to get some more information. Another term for this is a Deficiency Letter, which better indicates why these are dreaded.
Root Cause	The very, very, very underlying reason why something went wrong, typically the ultimate goal of a deviation investigation.
Safety	How safe the drug is.
Screening	Examining many thousands of compounds to find those with a potential effect on your chosen target.
Shelf Life	How long the product can be left on the shelf.
Shelf Life Specification	The specifications which must be met while sitting on the shelf.
Spin-off Company	A company started by an academic institution or academic researcher with the intention of commercialising a discovery made during basic research.
Stability Study	The process of leaving a number of samples on the shelf for a long period of time to ensure that the product degrades in the expected manner.
Standard Operating Procedure	A set of rules to ensure that processes are performed the same way every time.
Sterilisation	Killing everything! Everything microbial, at least.
Sterilisation Assurance Level	The probability that a sterilisation run will fail and leave living microbes behind.
Target	The protein or biological process which you want to change so as to cure or alleviate a disease.

Terminal Sterilisation	Producing the drug product in a clean but not aseptic fashion, then sterilising the final sealed product via heat or irradiation. Usually not appropriate for biological therapeutics.
Treatment Arm	A group of clinical patients who are receiving a specific treatment, different arms normally receive different drugs or dosages.
Trending	Checking to see if testing results, even if still within specifications, are drifting towards being out-of-specification.
Validation	Checking your processes to see if they consistently work as they should.
Worst-Case Load	Used in autoclave validation, this is a full load of difficult-to-sterilise objects.

About the Author

Originally from the sunny shores of Australia, CF Harrison currently works in the beer-filled heart of Bavaria. With a PhD in biochemistry, he has worked in drug discovery, as a scientific consultant, and as a regulatory affairs manager for a major international pharmaceutical company.

After being asked many, many times about the confusing world of the pharmaceutical industry, he decided to answer these questions once and for all – and thus this introductory book was born. Those interested in contacting him can drop a line to lifeafterlifescience@harrison-scientific.com.

Books in the series

Starting out in the Pharma industry: Essential knowledge for life scientists

CF Harrison, available in eBook and Paperback via Amazon

Pharmaceutical Regulatory Affairs: An Introduction for Life Scientists

CF Harrison, available in eBook and Paperback via Amazon

Aseptic Production: An Introduction for Life Scientists

CF Harrison, available in eBook and Paperback via Amazon